# Discovering Cities
## Sheffield

**H Doug Watts**
University of Sheffield

**Series Editors**
Peter S. Fox and
Christopher M. Law

Geographical Association

# Discovering Cities Sheffield

# Preface

The variety and complexity of cities as revealed in their built form has been a source of fascination to the local resident and visitor alike. Can a clear spatial structure be discerned? Why do activities cluster in distinctive quarters or zones? How do relict features throw light on the constantly evolving city?

For a long time, human geographers, regional economists, urban sociologists and local historians have sought to understand the processes which shape the city. The growth (or decline) of the city is affected by local, regional and global economic forces. The forces which shape the internal structure of the city are many and varied. There is a market in land that influences the pattern of land use and change. Public policies are often significant but can be complex to understand and difficult to follow. Social factors such as those of class and ethnic community identities are also important.

Written by urban geographers with vast knowledge and experience of the city in question, *Discovering Cities* gathers these issues together in concise and practical guides, illustrated with colour maps and photographs, to enable an enhanced perspective of cities of the British Isles.

**Peter S. Fox,** Chilwell Comprehensive School, Chilwell, Nottingham

**Christopher M. Law,** Visiting Fellow, University of Salford, and Research Associate, University of Gloucestershire

## Acknowledgements

The main sources upon which this account is based are listed in the bibliography. Other sources include a range of local and often ephemeral publications collected whilst living in Sheffield for over 30 years. A special thanks to both editors and to Gordon Dabinett and Jane Ferretti who read the early drafts and suggested a number of valuable changes.

© H Doug Watts, 2004

This book is copyright under the Berne Convention. All rights are reserved. Apart from any fair dealing for the purpose of private study, research, criticism or review, as permitted under the Copyright, Designs and Patents Act 1988, no part of this publication may be reproduced, stored in a retrieval system, or transmitted in any form or by any means, electronic, electrical, chemical, mechanical, optical, photocopying, recording or otherwise, without the prior written permission of the copyright owner. Enquiries should be addressed to the Geographical Association. The author has licensed the Geographical Association to allow members to reproduce material for their own internal school/departmental use, provided that the author holds the copyright.

ISBN 1 84377 114 4
First published 2004
Impression number 10 9 8 7 6 5 4 3 2 1
Year 2007 2006 2005

Published by the Geographical Association, 160 Solly Street, Sheffield S1 4BF.
Website: www.geography.org.uk
E-mail: ga@geography.org.uk

The Geographical Association is a registered charity: no 313129.

The Publications Officer of the GA would be happy to hear from other potential authors who have ideas for geography books. You may contact the Officer via the GA at the address above. The views expressed in this publication are those of the author and do not necessarily represent those of the Geographical Association.

Editing: Rose Pipes
Design and typesetting: Arkima, Dewsbury
Cartography: Paul Coles
Printing and binding: Emirates Printing Press, Dubai

# Contents

| | |
|---|---|
| Introduction | 6 |
| **The industrial city** | |
| Site, situation and early growth | 8 |
| Industrialisation | 10 |
| Suburbanisation | 13 |
| The central area | 17 |
| **The post-industrial city** | |
| Economic geographies | 20 |
| Social geographies | 28 |
| **Small area studies and trails** | |
| Introduction | 34 |
| Trail 1: Retailing and the heart of the city | 34 |
| Trail 2: City centre transect: zones in transition | 40 |
| Trail 3: The Lower Don Valley | 46 |
| Bibliography and further information | 51 |

Discovering Cities Sheffield

# Introduction

Sheffield, with a population of 513,000 in 2001, is one of the five largest cities in the UK. Once one of the country's main manufacturing centres, the city has had to meet major challenges posed by the decline of employment in its traditional industries – in particular the steel industry. Over the last two decades, investment in the city has led to major developments such as a large-scale regional shopping centre, a 30km-long light rail system, a 12,000-seat events arena, an international swimming pool, a national ice centre, an athletics stadium, a major art gallery and a Winter Garden. It is also home to two universities and the offices of several national government organisations as well as large companies such as HSBC and Norwich Union.

Twenty-first century Sheffield is only very slightly more dependent on manufacturing than Great Britain as a whole (in 2001 accounting for 16% of employment compared with the national average of 14%) and its economy is dominated by the service sector. Unemployment levels in mid-2003 remained above the national average, at 3.6% compared with the average 2.6%, but Sheffield is actively re-positioning itself to become a successful, distinctive city of European significance. It provides an excellent geographical example of the ways in which older industrial centres are adapting themselves to the needs of the present century.

Sheffield is just over two hours north of London by rail and is approximately equidistant from Leeds (to the north), Manchester (to the west) and Nottingham (to the south). It is linked to the motorway network by the M1 which runs through the north-east of the city. Good international connections are provided by the M18 link to the Humber ports and there is a frequent rail service to Manchester International Airport which lies within $1-1^1/_2$ hours drive from Sheffield. Local business interests, however, continue to press for better road links to the west.

Sheffield is the second city in the Yorkshire and the Humber Region (Leeds is the regional capital) and the dominant centre of the South Yorkshire sub-region, with the three smaller administrative areas of Rotherham (population 248,000), Barnsley (218,000) and Doncaster (287,000) making up the remainder (Figure 1). South Yorkshire's overall population of 1.3 million makes it comparable in size to Merseyside and Tyne and Wear. Within South Yorkshire, Sheffield is surrounded by a greenbelt except to the east where the built-up area continues without a break into Rotherham. In the west the city boundary includes part of the Peak District National Park. Although generally considered a northern city, the southern suburbs are adjacent to Derbyshire in the East Midlands. From 1974 to 1986 Sheffield was a Metropolitan

## Introduction

Figure 1: Sheffield and the South Yorkshire sub-region.

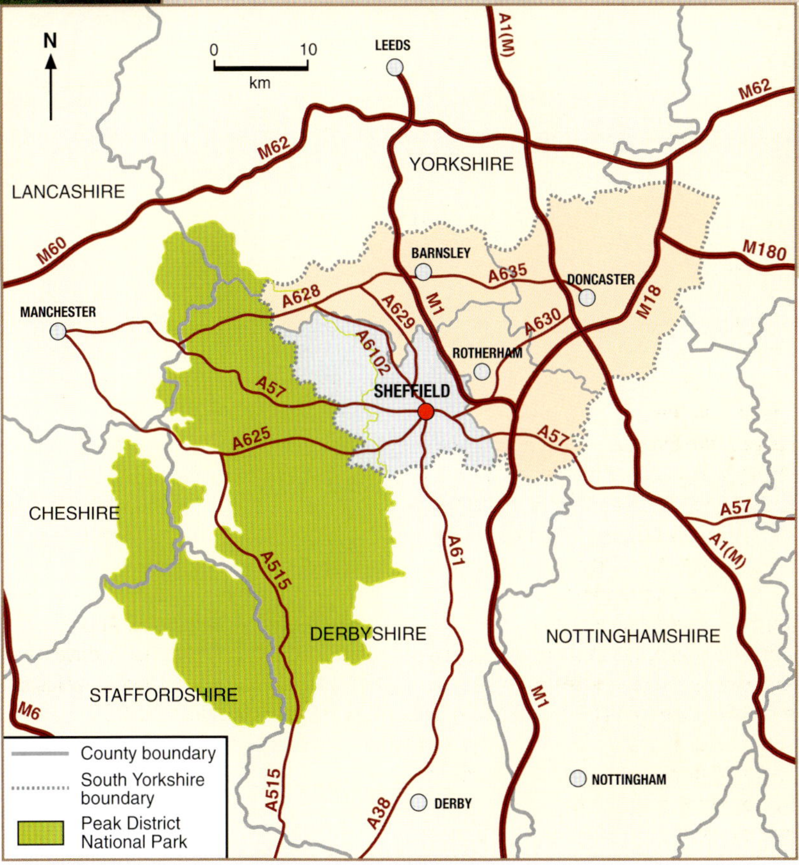

District within the larger South Yorkshire (Metropolitan) County. A number of organisations still operate within a South Yorkshire framework (police, ambulance, fire and rescue, passenger transport authorities) with representatives from Sheffield on their governing bodies, but for most purposes Sheffield City Council is the local administrative body. Historically, the city was part of the West Riding of Yorkshire and, before that, it was part of an area known as Hallamshire, a name recalled in a number of local institutions such as Sheffield Hallam University and the Royal Hallamshire Hospital.

The sections which follow begin with an overview of the evolution of the city up to the end of the 1970s and then focus on issues of policy and planning over the last 25 years, with an emphasis on the regeneration of the local economy over the last decade. Three trails provide detailed geographies of the central areas of the city and the Lower Don Valley. Data relate to the area administered by Sheffield City Council but, for reasons of space, the general discussion excludes the High Green/Chapeltown and Stocksbridge areas to the north of the main built-up area of the city (Figure 2).

Discovering Cities Sheffield

# The industrial city

*Figure 2: Sheffield: Site and situation.*

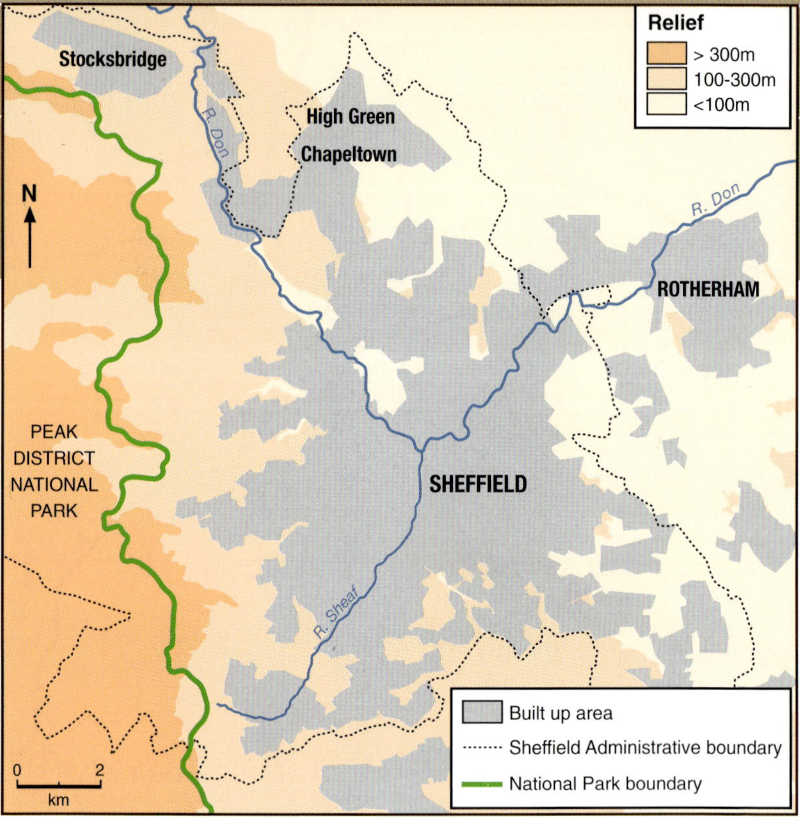

## Site, situation and early growth

Sheffield is situated on the eastern slopes of the Pennines at the western limits of the Middle and Lower Coal Measures which formed the basis of the South Yorkshire coalfield. The western boundary of the city reaches 458m above sea level while to the east, on the boundary with Rotherham (Figure 2), the city is only 30m above sea level – a variation in height which is unique for a large British city.

The town originated at the confluence of the River Sheaf (from which the town takes its name) and the River Don (Figure 3). The Don Valley falls into two distinct sections. The Upper Don (north-west of the confluence with the Sheaf) occupies a quite narrow valley with limited scope for development on the valley floor. The Lower Don (to the north-east) occupies a broad flat-bottomed valley which provided space for housing and industrial development, especially in the nineteenth century. The Pennine slopes are dissected by a number of smaller rivers which create areas of broken relief in the western parts of the city. Each of these river valleys brings a finger of green parkland close to the city centre. In these western parts of the city tree cover is extensive, giving the impression, especially in the summer months, of dense woodland interspersed with housing.

An Anglo-Saxon settlement at the confluence of the two rivers was

# The industrial city

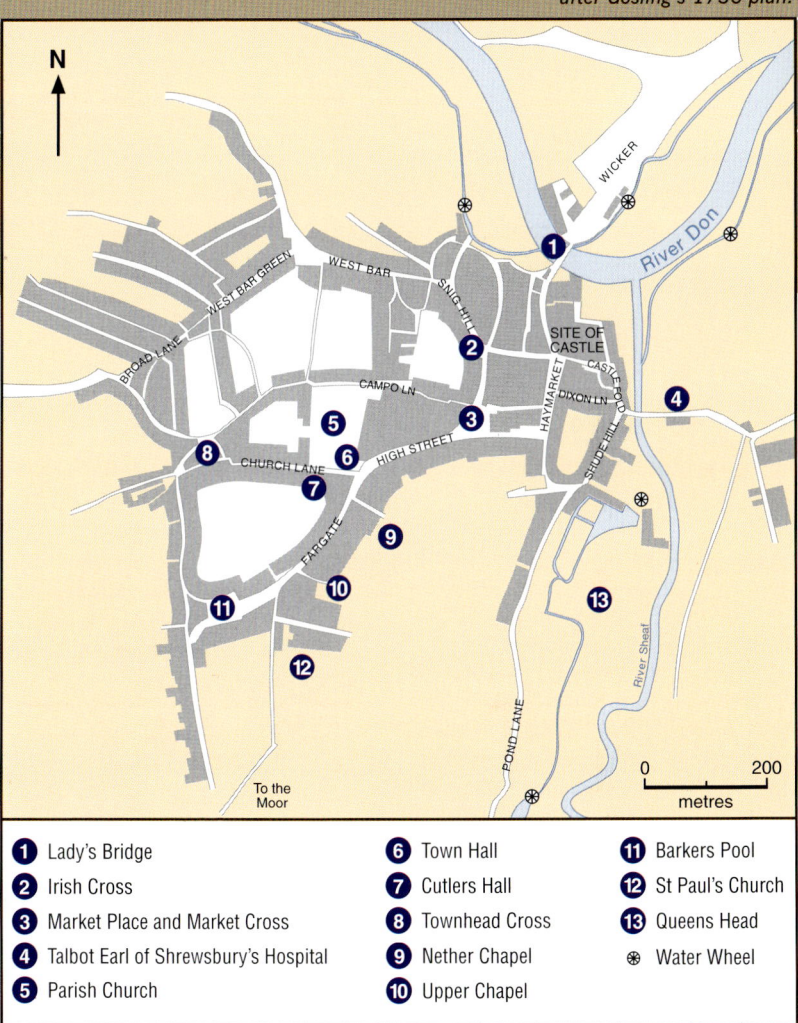

Figure 3: Mid-eighteenth century Sheffield, after Gosling's 1736 plan.

1. Lady's Bridge
2. Irish Cross
3. Market Place and Market Cross
4. Talbot Earl of Shrewsbury's Hospital
5. Parish Church
6. Town Hall
7. Cutlers Hall
8. Townhead Cross
9. Nether Chapel
10. Upper Chapel
11. Barkers Pool
12. St Paul's Church
13. Queens Head
✻ Water Wheel

replaced in the twelfth century by a wooden castle (later rebuilt in stone), defended by a moat on its south and west sides, and a small village alongside. From these early origins the town spread westwards to the parish church (now the Cathedral) which dates, in part, from the fifteenth century. Between parish church and castle the early town was centred upon the Market Place. There has been a remarkable continuity in land ownership in the city down to modern times with the land passing by family links through the Talbots (Earls of Shrewsbury) to (finally) the Howards (Dukes of Norfolk). A reminder of this continuity is the fact that over 300 local street names can be linked with the Norfolk family. Apart from these names and the Cathedral (with the medieval tombs of the fourth and sixth Earls of Shrewsbury) little remains of the medieval period. The castle was demolished in the mid-seventeenth century.

9

# Discovering Cities Sheffield

*Artist's impression of Sheffield Castle.*

## Industrialisation

Industrial activity and the growth of the city were closely related from a very early stage. The 1290s saw the granting of Sheffield's market charter and the first written reference to the production of metal goods in the city. From this very early start Sheffield became a distinctive metal-working industrial district made up of a cluster of related firms which obtained formal recognition in the setting up of the Company of Cutlers in Hallamshire in 1624. The development of the industrial district continued throughout the eighteenth and nineteenth centuries and by the 1840s Sheffield had become 'one great workshop for the production of cutlery and edge tools – a huge factory which scatters its separate departments in different parts of the town, but still retains them all, like so many links in a chain' (Wray *et al.*, 2001). Local resources played a major role in the early development of the industrial district. These included water power from the rivers, iron ore, coal and a hard local sandstone (Millstone Grit) which was used to produce the grinding wheels for sharpening edge tools such as knives, scissors, scythes and saws. However, the continued manufacture of metal products on an inland site owes little to natural resources and much to the high levels of technical innovation by steel producers and their willingness to adopt new technologies. Kelham Island Museum (see page 52) provides a detailed introduction to the economic and social history of the city.

By 1900 two distinct groups of industries were recognised in Sheffield: the lighter trades, concerned mainly with the production of small metal goods, and the heavy trades, largely associated with steel making and engineering. In 1911 the heavy trades employed nearly 40,000, the light trades 35,000. Although both trades used coal, coal mining was not an important activity within the city. The productive Middle Coal Measures were found only in the east where a small number of collieries operated in the 1900s. Handsworth, when it closed in 1966, was the last colliery within the city boundaries.

Although the most distinctive product of the lighter trades was cutlery they also

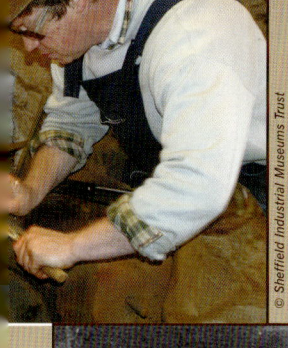

© Sheffield Industrial Museums Trust

*Hadfield's Steel Mill.*

© Sheffield Libraries Archive and Information; Local Studies

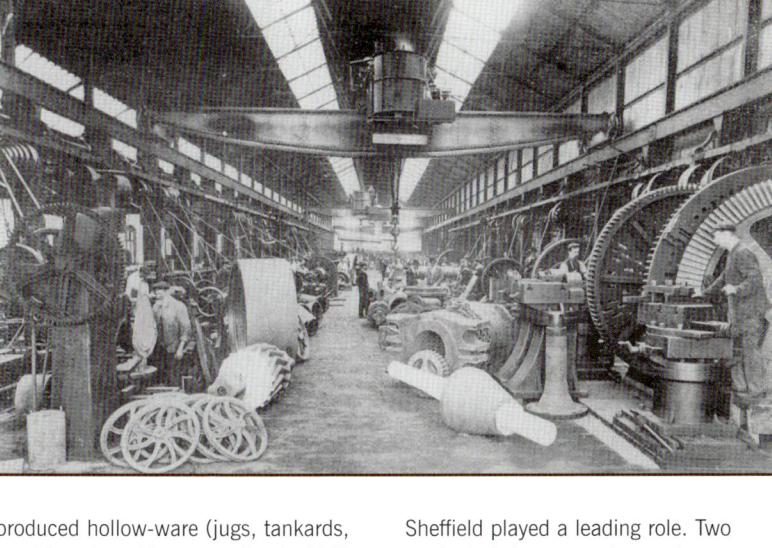

produced hollow-ware (jugs, tankards, bowls) and a wide range of tools (drills, scythes, razors, files, shears, scissors and saws). The production of cutting edges for use in machine tools was also regarded as part of these trades. Later the product range was widened beyond cutting tools to include garden tools and DIY products (such as hammers and screwdrivers). The lighter trades also included the production of consumer goods from silver and from cheaper metals such as Sheffield Plate (thin silver sheets on a copper base), pewter and electroplated silver. Within the cutlery industry there were numerous specialist activities (knife-handle makers, forgers, grinders) and a number of ancillary trades such as cutlery-case manufacturers. Initially the lighter trades were carried out in small workshops (by 'little mesters') but in some cases (especially from the 1830s onwards) the 'mesters' worked together in larger factory buildings, renting work space and power from the factory owner.

The heavy trades, which grew rapidly after the mid nineteenth century, were associated with the production of high quality steels in whose development Sheffield played a leading role. Two particularly important innovations were the development of manganese steel by Hadfield's (especially after the 1890s) and the rapid development of stainless steel production after the recognition of its special properties by a Sheffield man, Harry Brearley, just before the First World War. The quality of steels produced in Sheffield was enhanced further by competition and rivalry between local firms, especially in the armaments industry. Local stories tell how one firm (Firth) built shells and guns to burst the armour plate of another firm (Brown) who, in turn, produced stronger armour plate to withstand Firth's new shells. The adaptability of the steel makers, rather than their innovative abilities, was reflected in the adoption of electric arc furnaces to replace older steel-making technologies. Arc furnaces, developed in mainland Europe in the late nineteenth and early twentieth century, were firmly established in Sheffield by 1914, and by 1918 one of the Sheffield steelworks had probably the largest concentration of electric steel-melting capacity in the world.

# Discovering Cities Sheffield

*Bessamer Converter.*

Large-scale production of steel saw the beginning of the development of the Lower Don Valley as a major industrial area. This was encouraged further by the presence in the Lower Don of a canal and a branch from the main north-south rail line in Rotherham. By 1900 the Lower Don Valley included several large steel works and was a dense mass of steel furnaces, forging hammers, rolling mills and foundry casting shops under the ownership of large companies developed by local families. The industries created a smoke-filled atmosphere until Clean Air legislation took effect from 1956. As late as the 1980s, the sounds of steam hammers in the forges could still disturb sleep in some parts of Sheffield. Few of the Sheffield firms were simply steel producers but each formed the core of a heavy engineering complex. Although Sheffield was never characterised by large integrated iron and steel works, the factories were involved in the forging, rolling and casting of steel products, the production of wire, springs, railway track, capital equipment for the steel industry (such as steel works and rolling mills) and armoured steel plate for battleships.

By the mid twentieth century Sheffield's industries had a very distinctive geographical pattern. They formed a 'Y' shape, with the upper section of the 'Y' representing the Don and the lower section the Sheaf (Figure 4). The heavy trades were mainly located in the Lower Don Valley, the lighter trades in the Upper Don and the Sheaf Valleys. Steam power increasingly replaced water power, especially from 1830 onwards, thus freeing the small-scale industries from river valley locations. Significant numbers of workshops of the lighter trades were built on the ridges between the river valleys and a formed ring of activity around the central area of the city particularly to the west. However, unlike many cities, Sheffield does not

# The industrial city

*Figure 4: Patterns of industrial land use.
Source: Josvig, 1968.*

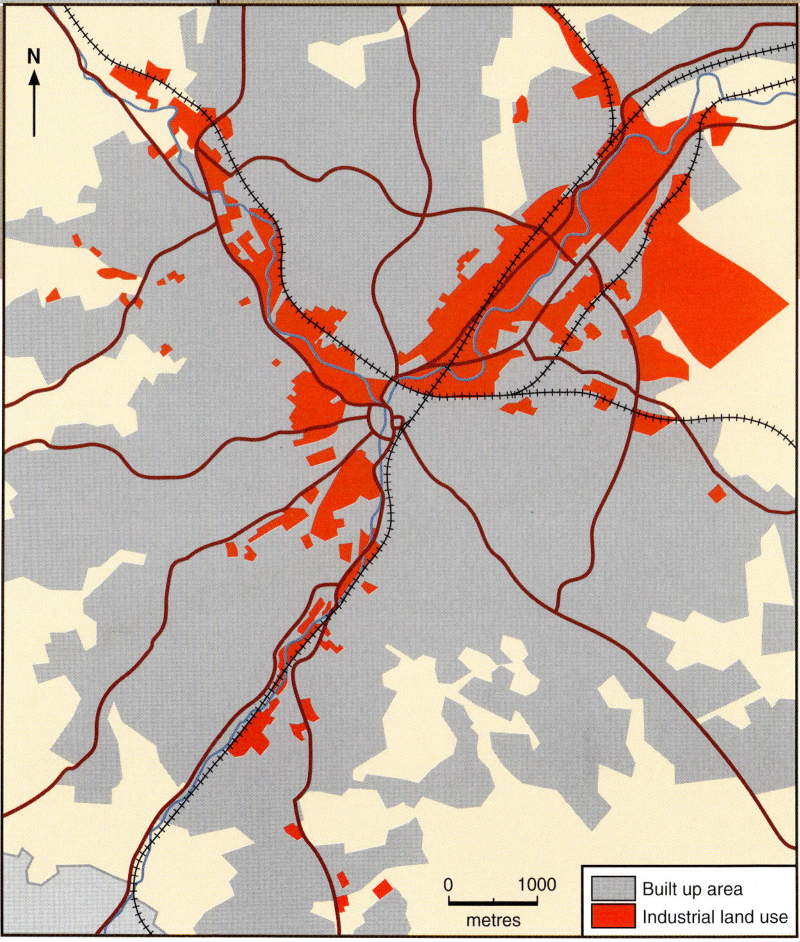

Built up area
Industrial land use

have a series of industrial estates surrounding the city – partly because the broken relief means that it does not have an outer ring road on the western side.

## Suburbanisation

Not surprisingly, the industrialisation of Sheffield was accompanied by major population growth (Table 1). From just under 50,000 in 1801 the population had increased by almost 100,000 by 1851 and by a further 250,000 between 1851 and 1901. Many of these people were migrants drawn from the rest of Yorkshire and neighbouring counties. There was very little long-distance migration into Sheffield in the nineteenth century. Population changes after 1901 are difficult to track because of adjustments to the city boundaries but the city had a population of almost half a million in 1921 and reached a peak of 538,000 in 1981. The only marked change in the pattern of population growth in the twentieth century was the arrival of a small number of immigrants from overseas in the post-war period. These came mainly from Pakistan and Commonwealth

# Discovering Cities Sheffield

*Housing the Steelworkers.*

territories in the Caribbean. Today, 9% of the population record themselves as members of ethnic minority groups, the largest group (3%) being of Pakistani origin.

Inevitably, with the growth of industry and population came the expansion of the residential areas of the city. Initially, outward expansion was controlled by the need to keep work and home in close proximity, but, following the introduction of horse trams from the 1870s and electric trams from the turn of the century, the extension of the residential areas proceeded rapidly.

The additional 250,000 people after 1851 were housed mainly on the eastern side of the city, especially in the Lower Don Valley where brick-built terraces abutted the new steel works. These were erected both by speculative builders and the steel companies. To the west some of the terraces were of stone. Back-to-back housing was less common in Sheffield than other industrial centres mainly because it was forbidden by a local bye law of 1864 which pre-dated the major expansion associated with the development of the heavy trades. It was in this second half of the nineteenth century that Sheffield's distinct social structure was created. While working-class housing was developed to the north and east the wealthier citizens were found in the western suburbs such as Broomhill and Ranmoor (Figure 5). The latter suburb was the choice of residence for two of the city's steel masters: Sir John Brown, who lived in Endcliffe Hall, and Mark Firth, who lived in Oakbrook. Both of these palatial houses were built in Ranmoor, well out of sight of the steel works in the east.

After the First World War the City Council played an increasingly dominant role in the expansion of the residential sector of the city. As the period between 1921 and 1951 saw little population growth, the Council's main aim was the rehousing of people from the older, high-

# The industrial city

Table 1: Population change in Sheffield 1801-2001. Sources: Binfield et al., 1993; Office for National Statistics. * Denotes boundary changes.

| Year | Population | Year | Population |
| --- | --- | --- | --- |
| 1801 | 46,000 | 1901 | 381,000 |
| 1821 | 62,000 | 1921* | 491,000 |
| 1841 | 111,000 | 1941 | No census |
| 1861 | 185,000 | 1961* | 494,000 |
| 1881 | 285,000 | 1981* | 538,000 |
|  |  | 2001 | 513,000 |

density properties in the central part of the city as part of a slum clearance policy. Major estates were built in the north at Shiregreen and Parson Cross and in the east in Manor. The Manor estate was built in the style of a 'garden city' with tree-lined avenues in geometrical street patterns and spaces reserved for schools, shops and churches. From 1919 to 1940 the Council built almost 27,000 dwellings – twice as many per 1000 population as the national average. Not all outward expansion was driven by the public sector and, especially in south-west Sheffield, private sector development of middle-class housing continued the long tradition begun by the steel masters, with the wealthier residents living to the west of the city. A good example of this kind of development is to be seen to the east and west of Ecclesall Road South.

Post-war developments saw further expansion of council housing. Much of this was associated with the City Council's decision to remove residential properties from the Lower Don Valley in order to achieve a clear separation between residential and industrial areas.

The most striking development in the immediate post-war period was Gleadless Valley on the edge of the city. It was started in 1955 and by the mid 1960s housed over 15,000 people in low-density housing. It was divided into three neighbourhoods (Rollestone, Herdings and Hemsworth) each with a school and shopping centre. The neighbourhoods are separated from each other by park or woodland. The gently rolling site gives this development a particularly attractive appearance.

In the inner parts of the city, tower blocks predominated, partly because of the lack of space for new low-rise housing within the city boundaries and also because of a general shift in the UK towards high-rise living in council estates. The inner city was also characterised by comprehensive redevelopment schemes. These involved total clearance of an area (often using compulsory purchase powers) and replacement by modern buildings and infrastructure. Large areas of nineteenth-century housing were removed in these schemes. Sharp lines can now been drawn across the urban map of Sheffield where the comprehensive redevelopment process came to an end in the 1970s and more emphasis was placed on the refurbishment of older properties.

The most significant development of this period in the central part of the city was the Park Hill estate built between 1956 and 1961 immediately to the east of the railway station in an area in which clearance and redevelopment had begun in 1936. It was argued that these inner sites would provide ready access to the city centre for jobs, shops and leisure facilities which were markedly lacking

# Discovering Cities Sheffield

*Figure 5: Sheffield's inner city and suburban areas.*

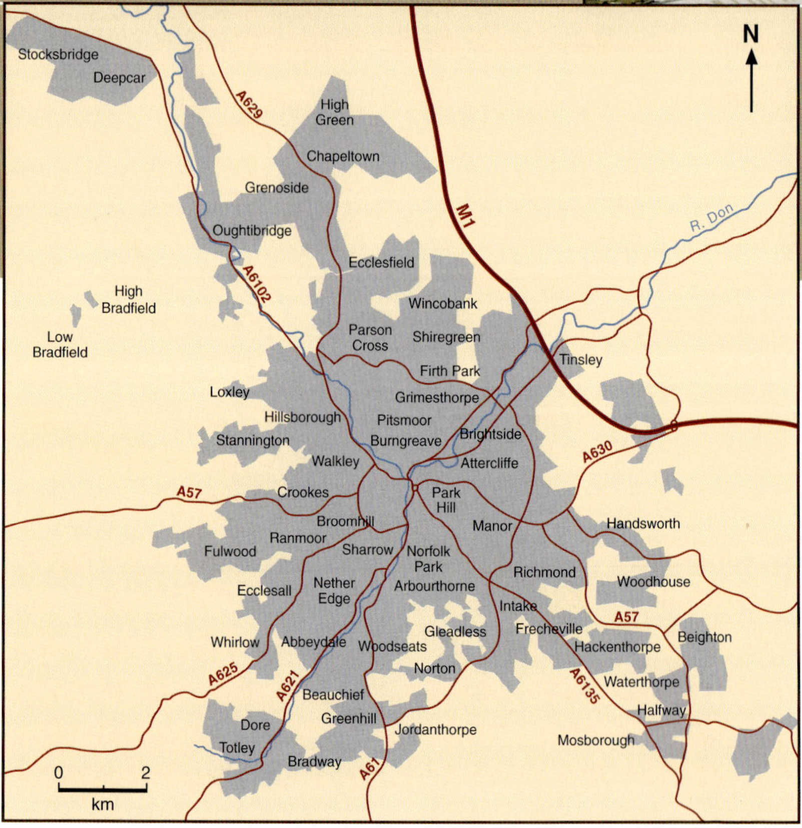

in many out-of-centre estates. At Park Hill almost 1000 flats and maisonettes were designed to house around 3000 people. The flats were linked by walkways, publicised as 'streets in the sky', along which deliveries could be made, children could play and housewives (sic) could chat. The whole complex (given listed status in 1998) covers some 13ha, making it one of the largest listed buildings in Britain. Subsequently, Hyde Park flats were built to house another 5000 people in the area to the east of Park Hill. The central sections of the Hyde Park complex dominated the Sheffield skyline for almost 40 years. Other developments included Netherthorpe/Upperthorpe to the north-west of the city (begun in 1959), Burngreave to the north (begun 1960) and Norfolk Park (begun in 1962). The latter, consisting primarily of 16-storey towers, was as dramatic a part of the cityscape as Hyde Park flats. By 1981 the Council owned 45% of the dwellings in the city, one of the highest proportions of council ownership in the UK.

Boundary constraints, which had restricted the outward expansion of the city, were removed in 1967 when Sheffield took over part of northern Derbyshire and began the development of Mosborough, which was referred to as Sheffield's 'new town'. This, like the earlier Gleadless development, was divided into a series of townships but with a mix of council and private housing. Attempts were made to mix

# The industrial city

Suburban housing, Nether Edge.

the council and private sector in medium-sized blocks, to avoid large estates, but this proved difficult to achieve. Initial developments were slow but Mosborough now has its own major district shopping centre, Crystal Peaks.

## The central area

The late nineteenth-century expansion of the city saw major re-organisation of the central area and the development of offices, retailing and buildings linked to the administration of the city. The Victorian rebuilding of the central area reflected the needs of a much larger city and saw the removal of poor quality housing and its replacement by public buildings and commercial activities. The early nineteenth-century housing was at very high density – one street 137 metres long contained 40 workshops, 192 houses and 800 residents. In the commercial core, shopping streets (such as High Street and Fargate) were widened and major public buildings constructed. Much of the Victorian city centre was destroyed in the Second World War (Figure 6). Damage here was more extensive than in the industrial areas of the Don Valley and locals claimed the bombers mistook the Sheaf Valley and its environs for the Don. Most of the major department stores were destroyed.

The rebuilt retail area of the 1950s and 1960s consisted of two main self-contained shopping zones (the Castle and the Moor). The city at that time claimed it had more department stores than any other city north of London. This was because major retailers (such as Marks and Spencer) each had two stores, one in each shopping zone. The existence of the two zones made the

# Discovering Cities Sheffield

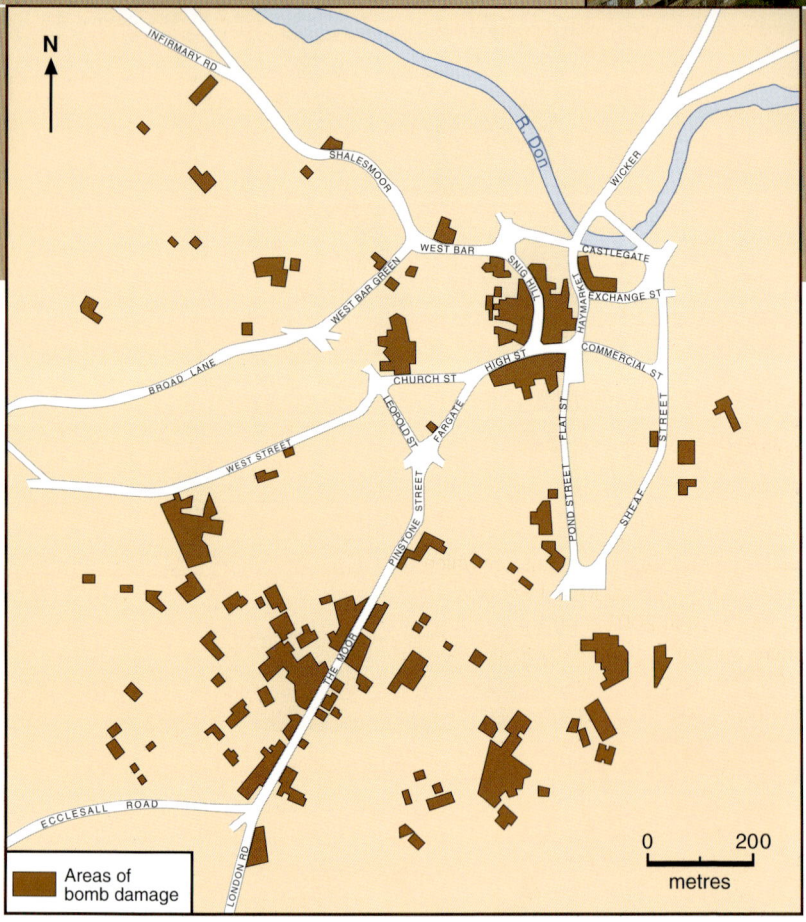

Figure 6: Bomb damage from the Second World War. Source: Josvig, 1968.

core of the centre difficult to define. This has presented a particular challenge for urban renewal at the present time.

In the mid 1970s Sheffield was a prosperous manufacturing centre with unemployment levels below the national average. It was a highly specialised city at the centre of an important metal-working industrial district. The City Council had a reputation for pioneering housing developments such as Park Hill and Gleadless Valley. Few would have guessed that over the next 30 years this pattern would change dramatically.

The late 1970s saw the beginning of a traumatic time for Sheffield. Between 1981 and 2001 the population of the city fell by 25,000 and in 1983 unemployment moved above the national average. The declining performance of the Sheffield economy was mainly a reflection of problems in its manufacturing sector. De-industrialisation (reflecting a fall in the numbers employed in manufacturing as well as a decline in the relative importance of manufacturing to the city's economy) was dramatic. Table 2 provides a broad indication of employment trends. Changes in industrial classifications and boundaries

# The industrial city

Table 2: Sheffield employment change, 1971-2001
Sources: based on Sheffield City Council and Office for National Statistics Annual Business Inquiry, 2001.

|  | 1971 | 1981 | % change 1971-81 | 1991 | % change 1981-91 | 2001 | % change 1991-2001 |
|---|---|---|---|---|---|---|---|
| All manufacturing | 136,000 | 92,000 | -32% | 56,000 | -39% | 36,000 | -36% |
| All manufacturing (% of all employment) | 49 | 37 |  | 25 |  | 16 |  |
| Metal products and basic metal manufacturing | 90,000 | 42,000 | -53% | 20,000 | -52% | 17,000 | -15% |
| Metal products and basic metal manufacturing (% of all employment) | 33 | 17 |  | 8 |  | 7 |  |
| Services | 140,000 | 157,000 | 12% | 170,000 | 8% | 194,000 | 14% |
| Services (% of all employment) | 51 | 63 |  | 75 |  | 84 |  |

of statistical units make precise comparisons difficult. Table 2 excludes employment in the primary sector which employed around 5000 in 1971 and under 1000 in 2001. In the mid 1970s there were more than 20 factories with 1000 employees or more; now fewer than five have this characteristic.

The Lower Don Valley was hit particularly badly. By 1988 40% of the available land was vacant, derelict or underused, and employment in the area had fallen from 40,000 in 1975 to 13,000. An unforeseen advantage of the loss of the very largest factories, such as the steel works of Hadfield's, Brown Bayley and Tinsley Park, was that they offered significant areas of land (under a single land owner) suitable for large-scale redevelopment after reclamation and clearance. Economic difficulties were paralleled by concerns about housing quality in Sheffield. Many of the pre- and post-war council-built properties presented severe structural, social and environmental problems, leading, in some cases, to demolition. The early 1980s were challenging times for the city as it attempted to find a way forward.

Discovering Cities Sheffield

# The post-industrial city

*Showroom.*

© Russell Skidmore/Showroom & Workstation

## Economic geographies

### Policy responses to de-industrialisation

It took some time for the city to respond to the rapid collapse in employment in the manufacturing sector. In part this reflected local hostility from Labour-controlled Sheffield to Conservative Government initiatives such as Enterprise Zones (none were ever set up in Sheffield). The situation was not helped by the fact that economic development matters were dealt with by both South Yorkshire County Council (SYCC) and Sheffield City Council until the abolition of SYCC in 1986. Furthermore, in the early 1980s the private and public sectors had contrasting and, at times, conflicting agendas. As a result the first regeneration activities were led by the City Council. These included the development of Science and Technology Parks and the designation of a Cultural Industries Quarter (see Trail 2, pages 40-45). The City Council has also played a major role (with the private sector) in the creation of the retail and leisure developments in the Devonshire Quarter (see Trail 1, pages 34-39).

A greater spirit of partnership had developed by the late 1980s and co-operation was strengthened by plans to hold the World Student Games in the city in 1991. It was hoped this 'flagship event' would change the image of the city and provide the basis for regeneration around the theme of 'City of Sport'. The decision was not without its critics (costs were thought to be excessive in relation to the benefits) and the pros and cons of hosting the event are still debatable. Although not widely acknowledged, the Games were successful on a local level but, with an essentially hostile media and with negligible interest from central government, they did little to change the city's image. Nevertheless, they led to a marked capital investment in international-standard sporting facilities, especially in the Lower Don Valley (see Trail 3, pages 46-50).

The partnership between the private and public sectors became closer (if not always without differences of opinion) when the Conservative Government set up the Sheffield Development Corporation (SDC) in 1988. Despite its title, the SDC was concerned only with the Lower Don Valley, excluding the areas developed as the leisure facilities for the World Student Games. The SDC had a grant of £60 million from central government to kick-start private sector developments and became the planning

# The post-industrial city

*Supertram.*

authority for its area between 1988 and 1997. The main outcome of the SDC's activities during its nine-year life was the preparation of the infrastructure of the Don Valley for redevelopment. Major land-reclamation schemes were undertaken (much of the land was badly polluted from industrial use), land holdings were brought together to create large development sites and a dual carriageway was constructed down the middle of the valley. Certainly much of the Lower Don Valley is now filled with new premises replacing the derelict land of the late 1980s and early 1990s. Although the new industrial units were welcomed by the city, there was some tension between the city and the SDC over the extent of retail, office and leisure developments within the SDC area (Trail 3) which it was thought would hit the vitality of the city centre.

In other parts of the city, where planning was still controlled by the City Council, there were significant improvements to the infrastructure, partly in order to stimulate the local economy. Major developments included the Mosborough Parkway to provide a new road link between the city centre and residential developments to the south (Figure 7). The major development in public transport was completion of the Supertram system in 1995. Three lines from north, east and south link the out-of-centre shopping areas at Meadowhall (a major regional shopping mall), Crystal Peaks (in Mosborough) and Hillsborough (an older centre to the north of the city) with the city centre. The tram system has not been as successful as that in Manchester and use is still below the predicted levels but, after a hesitant start, it now carries 11 million passengers per year.

Admittedly there were some false starts in these years. The most dramatic was the National Centre for Popular Music (see Trail 2, pages 40-45) development funded mainly by National Lottery money, a disappointing initiative that closed after a very short life. Despite being a distinctive building, as a tourist attraction it was too small to be a major visitor destination and the content came in for criticism. Similarly, attempts to develop a city airport, with international connections to Europe, on the site of the former Tinsley Park steelworks, were not successful (Figure 7). The last regular scheduled flights were withdrawn in 2002, though the airfield remains operational for private flights, and the surrounding area is rapidly developing as a major new business park.

At the present time all the main actors in the city's economy (together with social and community organisations) are linked together within a Local Strategic Partnership (LSP) called SheffieldFirst. A sign of the spirit of co-operation in the city is that this was one of the first LSPs to be set up in the UK. It is within the LSP that an urban regeneration

# Discovering Cities Sheffield

*Figure 7: Sheffield's transport infrastructure.*

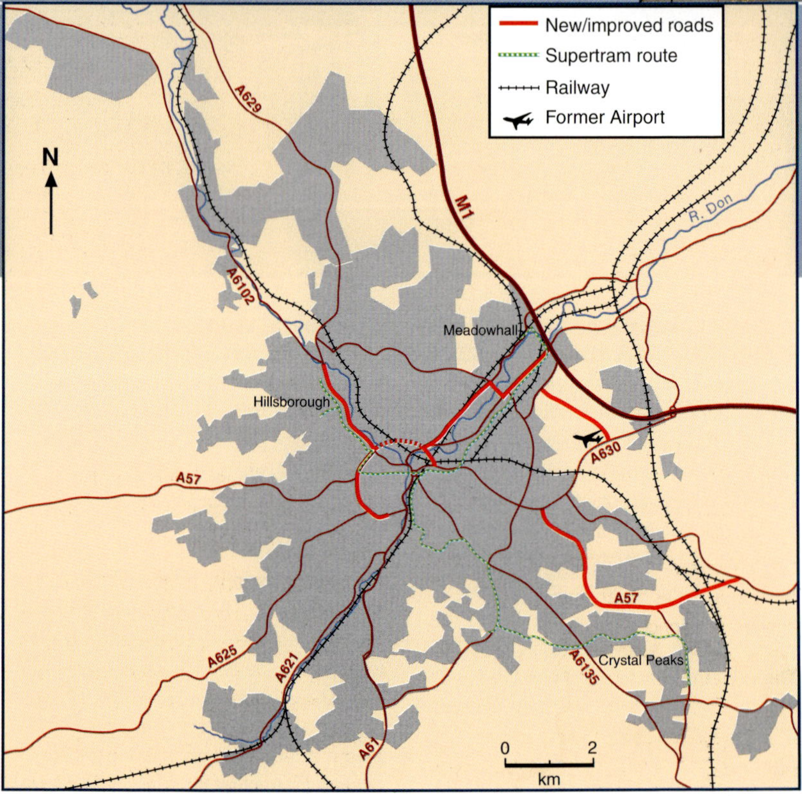

company (Sheffield 1) is driving investment in the physical infrastructure of the city, an activity seen most clearly in the Heart of the City Project (Trail 1). Although Sheffield was eligible only for small amounts of EU regional aid from the mid 1980s (some was used in the construction of World Student Games facilities), developments at local level have been aided since 2000 when the EU recognised Sheffield as part of the South Yorkshire Objective 1 area. Only one other major urban area in the UK (Merseyside) has similar status.
Objective 1 areas have a GDP of less than 75% of the EU average. Sheffield's GDP is probably better than this (estimated at about 82%) but the overall figure for South Yorkshire is pulled down by the other three administrative areas in the sub-region. Objective 1 status has opened up major new sources of funding for the regeneration of the city's economic and social structures, led to a wider recognition of the roles of small- and medium-sized enterprises in the regeneration process, and highlighted the potential for e-commerce and e-learning to drive the revival of a city economy.

Despite some minor setbacks, there is little doubt that the economy of Sheffield has changed over the last 20 years, though the extent to which local and national policies have made a difference is open to debate. It is difficult to separate out the influence of local activities from the wider national changes within which they are set. A careful evaluation of the impacts of these policies is a task for the future but there is little doubt that the city of

# The post-industrial city

Meadowhall.

2004 is very different from the highly industrialised city of 30 years ago. It has moved from a city based primarily on production to one based increasingly on the provision of business and consumer services.

## The contemporary economy

Service sector activities provided over 80% of the jobs in Sheffield in 2001. Many of these jobs are associated with the provision of local services such as education, local government and health services. However, over the last three decades, Sheffield has also come to provide business and consumer services to the rest of the UK through the branches of major public and private sector organisations. Despite this, and the strength of Meadowhall as a regional shopping centre, in contrast to similar-sized cities such as Leeds and Manchester, Sheffield provides relatively few regional administrative and business services. In part, this is due to Leeds being the regional capital for the Yorkshire and Humber region.

Business and consumer services serving mainly non-local markets encompass a range of activities including retailing, higher education and research, national government administration, financial services, call centres and the provision of leisure facilities. There are also signs of an expanding legal service, with a number of major law firms.

Despite the growth in service sector employment, manufacturing still makes a major contribution to the city's economy, although, as shown on page 19, it is much less significant than 30 years ago.

**Retailing,** based on the Meadowhall shopping centre, has made Sheffield one of the major centres of the north of England. Meadowhall's competitors in the regional shopping-centre market are the MetroCentre in north-east England, Trafford Park in the north-west and Merry Hill in the West Midlands. Planning restrictions on out-of-centre developments make it unlikely that any further regional shopping centres will emerge to challenge Meadowhall's role in this part of the UK. It currently employs over 7000 people at peak periods, although many are on part-time contracts.

Meadowhall provides a classic example of the importance of local entrepreneurship in economic growth. It was promoted by two property developers – Eddie Healey and Paul Sykes (reminiscent of the activities of Brown and Firth in the steel industry in

# Discovering Cities Sheffield

Fargate.

the nineteenth century). Sheffield City Council took the adventurous step of granting planning permission even though the new centre would clearly challenge the city's central shopping area. It would have been difficult to refuse permission because the developers had significant land holdings elsewhere in South Yorkshire and refusal might have led to the construction of the centre outside Sheffield. The site (the former Hadfield's steel works) is highly accessible. It is adjacent to (and visible from) the M1 and at the junction of rail lines linking the four largest towns of South Yorkshire. It was subsequently linked into the tram and bus systems through its own interchange. While successful in itself as a shopping centre, Meadowhall has never managed to attract related leisure facilities (other than a multi-screen cinema) and there have been concerns in Sheffield about its impact on the city centre.

The relationships between Meadowhall and the city centre are difficult to define, but there is little doubt that the fortunes of the city centre have been hit by the diversion of business to Meadowhall. In the early years after Meadowhall's opening in 1990 it was estimated that it had taken about 20% of the city centre business. Sheffield's main Marks and Spencer store is now in Meadowhall, with a smaller operation in the city centre, and House of Fraser shut its city centre store after the opening of its Meadowhall branch. The City Council monitors developments at Meadowhall and considers their impact on the city centre. As an example, permission to extend Marks and Spencer facilities at Meadowhall was conditional on the addition of another floor in their city centre store.

In the city centre the two-centred shopping area is giving way to a retail core concentrated increasingly in the central part (Fargate, Pinstone Street and Barker's Pool) of the linear shopping area. This trend is being encouraged by local planning initiatives which envisage a new retail quarter linking Barker's Pool and the Moor. Both ends of the linear shopping area are characterised by smaller chain stores and it has still not been possible to identify a new role for the northern end (see Trail 2). Unlike Newcastle, where the central shopping area was redeveloped before the opening of the MetroCentre, shoppers in Sheffield city centre face a rather unexciting 1950s and 1960s shopping experience. The only significant changes since 1970 have been the construction of Orchard Square at the southern end of Fargate, the pedestrianisation of a number of the main shopping streets and the emergence of Devonshire Green as a specialist shopping area. Of course, the city centre shopping experience owes much to the nature of the urban landscape.

# The post-industrial city

University of Sheffield.

This is now changing rapidly with the implementation of the Heart of the City project (see Trail 1).

**Higher education and research** in the city, unlike retailing, looks particularly to national and international markets. The University of Sheffield (5400 employees) and Sheffield Hallam University (3300 employees) are among the largest employers in the city and play a vital role in its economy. Their 36,000 full-time students (including over 6000 from overseas) draw large sums of public and private money into the city. Student spending has stimulated the growth of important leisure facilities in the city, including an active night scene. In addition to the multipliers resulting from student spending, universities make other significant contributions to the local economy. The University of Sheffield alone brings £90.8 million a year into the city in the form of research income. If this research was a stand-alone activity the turnover would place it amongst the largest Sheffield-based firms. In addition to employment generated from research funding, the universities have stimulated the creation of new firms and have helped to attract new activities to the city.

Higher education and research facilities have been well-established in Sheffield for many years. This is in contrast to the other service sectors, many of which have emerged as important parts of the city economy only recently, even though the roots of such service sector growth can be traced back to the late 1970s and early 1980s.

**National government administration** arrived in the form of a major government department, the Manpower Services Commission, in 1980. This formed part of the dispersal of the civil service from London initiated by the Labour Government of the 1970s. The dispersal was a response to rising costs in London and a desire to cut public expenditure. The successors of this large government department still remain in Sheffield – there are major national offices of Jobcentre Plus, the Department for Work and Pensions, the Home Office and the Department for Education and Skills (see Trail 2). More recently, Sheffield has been selected by the government as the home of the University for Industry, more widely known as Learn Direct. The presence of these government offices has also encouraged the location within the city of private sector support activities in fields such as data processing.

**Financial services** increased following the movement to the city of a significant number of jobs by Hong Kong & Shanghai Banking Corporation (HSBC). The bank was attracted particularly by

# Discovering Cities Sheffield

*HSBC's Sheffield Office in the Pennine Centre.*

the lack of competition for clerical labour (especially women) in a city dominated by employment opportunities for men in the steel industry. Typically, the head office remained in London. The arrival of HSBC (currently employing around 2000) was followed by Norwich Union who, on experiencing a shortage of labour in Norwich, selected Sheffield as its second major UK centre. A later addition to the financial services sector was the Abbey National bank, which currently employs around 1200. Although many of the dispersed jobs are concerned with routine rather than strategic tasks (much of the Abbey National and Norwich Union activities involve call centre work), there are exceptions in that the HSBC Sheffield offices contain one of only five global technology centres of the bank. The financial sector of the city is highly dependent on the continuing presence and success of these important financial companies. If any one of them decided to relocate or was in financial difficulties, it could result in hundreds of redundancies in the city.

**Call centres** have emerged as an important source of employment in many parts of the UK, including Sheffield, over the last decade. Accurate figures for total employment in Sheffield-based call centres are difficult to find, and may include an overlap with figures for the financial services. However, it is estimated that they account for 8000 jobs, albeit many are part-time and not well-paid. Sheffield's larger call centres include the customer support services of electrical retailer Dixons, the main call centre of Freemans catalogue company (see Trail 3) and Ant Marketing (see Trail 2). Smaller operations include those of William Hill (betting) and National Express (rail ticket sales and enquiries). With the exception of Ant Marketing, which is a local firm, all the others are branches of major firms who have selected Sheffield for their call centre operations. However, future employment in call centres may well be threatened by the trend to move the work to cheaper sites, especially in India. Competition from low-cost locations has already had an adverse impact on employment in some of Sheffield's traditional manufacturing industries, such as cutlery and hand-tool manufacture.

**Leisure facilities** (including sport and culture – see Trails 1-3) are encouraging the emergence of a café society. This trend is occurring perhaps rather later than in other British cities, but national and international chains are now establishing their presence in Sheffield. The marked increase in the number of

# The post-industrial city

The Assay Office.

hotel rooms in the city in recent years is an indication of the extent to which the sporting, cultural and social leisure facilities have attracted outside interest.

**Manufacturing** is still significant despite the dominance of the service sector in post-industrial Sheffield, though the particular manufacturing mix does not provide a strong basis for long-term future growth in employment. Most of the factories are survivors from the past and there has been very little expansion of employment arising from the establishment of new branch plants.

Manufacturing in Sheffield has two distinctive features. First, three-quarters of the manufacturing activity is concentrated in only five sectors, and second, four of those five sectors are closely related to older and traditional industries rather than modern, high-technology activities. However, although the products are traditional, it is sometimes forgotten that the Sheffield plants utilise modern technologies in their production processes. Metal production is over-represented four times compared with the national average. Sheffield is a major European centre for the production of stainless steel (made primarily from scrap metals in electric arc furnaces), but virtually all the engineering steels are now produced in the adjacent town of Rotherham. The Magna Centre (see page 52) in Rotherham provides a good introduction to modern steel making.

Metal goods are three times over-represented in the Sheffield economy, reflecting strengths in forging and casting (especially for the aerospace sector) and the production of tools, including items for the DIY market. Some elements of the cutlery industry remain (employing less than 1000) and related to this is the city's reputation for the manufacture of blades for use in surgical procedures. Specialist metals technologies are also used to produce orthopaedic implants such as hip joints. In the precious metals sector Sheffield remains as one of only four UK centres with an Assay Office, and it handles more than 40% of the UK business. Two other important manufacturing industries (engineering and food) are under-represented in the city, though Sheffield is an important UK centre for the manufacture of baggage-handling systems used at major international airports. Trebor Bassetts, producing liquorice allsorts and jelly babies, is now one of the largest factories in the city.

The decline in manufacturing employment has resulted in a change in the distribution of industry within the city. The Y-shaped pattern of the

# Discovering Cities Sheffield

Learndirect and Inland Revenue Offices, Moorfoot.

twentieth century (see Figure 4) is giving way to a T shaped pattern with the crossbar aligned along the M1 and the down stroke representing the Lower Don Valley. This eastward shift reflects the significance of motorway links to modern manufacturing activities and the activities of property developers along the M1 corridor – a corridor of development encouraged by local plans. The largest site is the Sheffield Business Park at the former airport.

### Future economic challenges

Despite the expansion of its service sector Sheffield still has a number of challenges to face. First, it is dependent to a large extent on the policies of a limited number of large organisations. Second, it has a branch-plant economy in which most of the major activities in both services and manufacturing are owned by firms with head offices outside the city. The fact that much of the economy is externally owned tends to reduce the commitment of firms to the local area and the involvement of management in local affairs. Third, despite the high profile success of one or two small- and medium-sized firms and some very successful property developments, Sheffield (like South Yorkshire as a whole) has one of the lowest rates of new firm formation in the UK. Fourth, it has not yet established a distinctive niche in the European city system. As the City Strategy observes,

'to sustain its existence as a major city it must perform one or more specialist roles that are not provided by the regional capital' (Sheffield City Council, 2003). What these specialist roles will be is still not clear.

## Social geographies

### Residential patterns

Over the last 30 years Sheffield City Council's role in housing provision has declined dramatically, as in most cities, reflecting changes in national housing policy. Also, the pattern of housing provision has moved from outward expansion to an emphasis on internal re-organisation.

New building by the Council came to a halt in 1991 and much of new social housing is now provided through housing associations. Today, the proportion of local authority housing is only just over a quarter, but still twice the national average (see Figure 8d). Almost 15,000 dwellings were sold under the right-to-buy legislation in the 1980s and stock was further reduced by the redevelopment of council estates, a process which, as is shown below, frequently involved demolition. For example, the Council demolished 2500 dwellings in the 1980s.

Internal re-organisation has taken a number of forms, all involving the

# The post-industrial city

*Netherthorpe Flats.*

redevelopment of urban (brownfield) sites. Many council high-rise blocks and some of the older council houses have been replaced by new housing and there has been a marked rise in city centre living, especially amongst students and young professionals.

In the council sector the showpiece developments of the 1950s and 1960s became the problem housing areas of the 1990s. Many of the earlier developments survive and have been refurbished, but the experience of the Park Hill flats is typical. The population of the complex is currently half that at the time it was opened. In 2003 around 10% of the homes were empty and for 40% of the tenants it was a stop-gap between other properties. Its future is currently under review. The unpopularity of similar developments has led to widespread demolition. The most striking changes to the city skyline resulted from the demolition of the central sections of the Hyde Park flats and the Norfolk Park tower blocks. In most cases, these sites have been redeveloped with low-rise housing. However, not all high-rise council housing was demolished, and some tower blocks, such as those at Netherthorpe, have been refurbished as part of wider housing regeneration projects.

The current fascination with city centre living is reflected in an increase in the population of the central area of Sheffield, in part with social housing, as at Broomhall, but also with upmarket apartments and student accommodation. Much of this is new build but others comprise converted former industrial and commercial premises. This process has been actively encouraged by the City Council. Private sector student accommodation tends to be found around the sites of the two universities, and the inner-city housing developments do not, as yet, form a coherent whole. New developments are adjacent to properties awaiting redevelopment and there are potential conflicts between the 24-hour entertainment scene and residential accommodation. This problem is recognised by the City Council who attempt to manage the conflict by monitoring the hours of the leisure facilities and insisting on high levels of sound-proofing in both leisure and residential properties.

Outside the central area there has been some continued development in the south-east at Mosborough, but the green belt and the Peak District National Park have limited the extent of outward expansion. However, re-organisation in the education and health sectors has freed up at least three major brownfield sites on the edge of the city. In the education sector, Sheffield Hallam University, following a strategy of concentrating activity on its two central sites, sold a large area for residential development in the south of the city at Totley. The former sites of Middlewood Hospital (to the north) and Lodge Moor

# Discovering Cities Sheffield

*Ecclesall Road South.*

Hospital (to the west) are two areas currently under development by the private sector.

## A polarised city

Overall, the changes in housing patterns have done little to alter Sheffield's long-established distinctive social structure. As mentioned earlier, in the late nineteenth century the owners of the steel mills lived in palatial mansions in western suburbs while the employees were clustered in terraced houses adjacent to the steel works in the east. The predominance of poorer neighbourhoods to the east and richer neighbourhoods to the west creates a geographically and socially divided city. Although other cities have marked variations in quality of life within their boundaries, Sheffield is unusual in that these variations take on such a marked geographical expression. Indeed, in this sense, Sheffield is one of the most polarised large cities in England.

The continuation of this striking internal structure with its marked contrasts reflects, in part, Sheffield's situation on the edge of the Peak District National Park. This has helped to make Sheffield a relatively self-contained city. Its compact character enables residents on the high ground to the west to look across the city to the farmland in the east. Indeed the attractive tree-lined suburbs to the west, in close proximity to the National Park, are amongst the wealthiest suburbs in Britain. In the 1970s and 1980s the middle class did not leave the city for dormitory suburbs outside its boundaries, as was the case in cities such as Leeds and Manchester. Effectively the National Park prevented the development of commuter villages in the Peak District.

Contrasts in the quality of life are highlighted in the Index of Multiple Deprivation (Figure 8). A high score on the Index reflects low incomes, restricted employment opportunities, poor health, limited education, poor housing and limited access to services such as a GP. Overall, deprivation in Sheffield is not as marked as that in cities such as Manchester and Nottingham, but some of its wards are among the 5% of most deprived in the UK: Southey Green, Burngreave and Manor are among the worst 1% in the UK (Figure 8a). Overall, in the east of the city most of the wards are in the 50% most deprived in the UK. In contrast, the wards to the west are in the 50% least deprived and two of them, Broomhill and Ecclesall, are ranked among the 5% of least deprived in England. Even more strikingly, only one other ward across all the major English cities is in this lowest 5%. These figures on multiple deprivation feed through into, for example, significant heath contrasts between east and west, with men and women in the west living on average

## The post-industrial city

*Figure 8: (a) Index of multiple deprivation – compared to UK average; (b) Unemployment figures for Sheffield. Source: Reid, 2001; Office for National Statistics.*

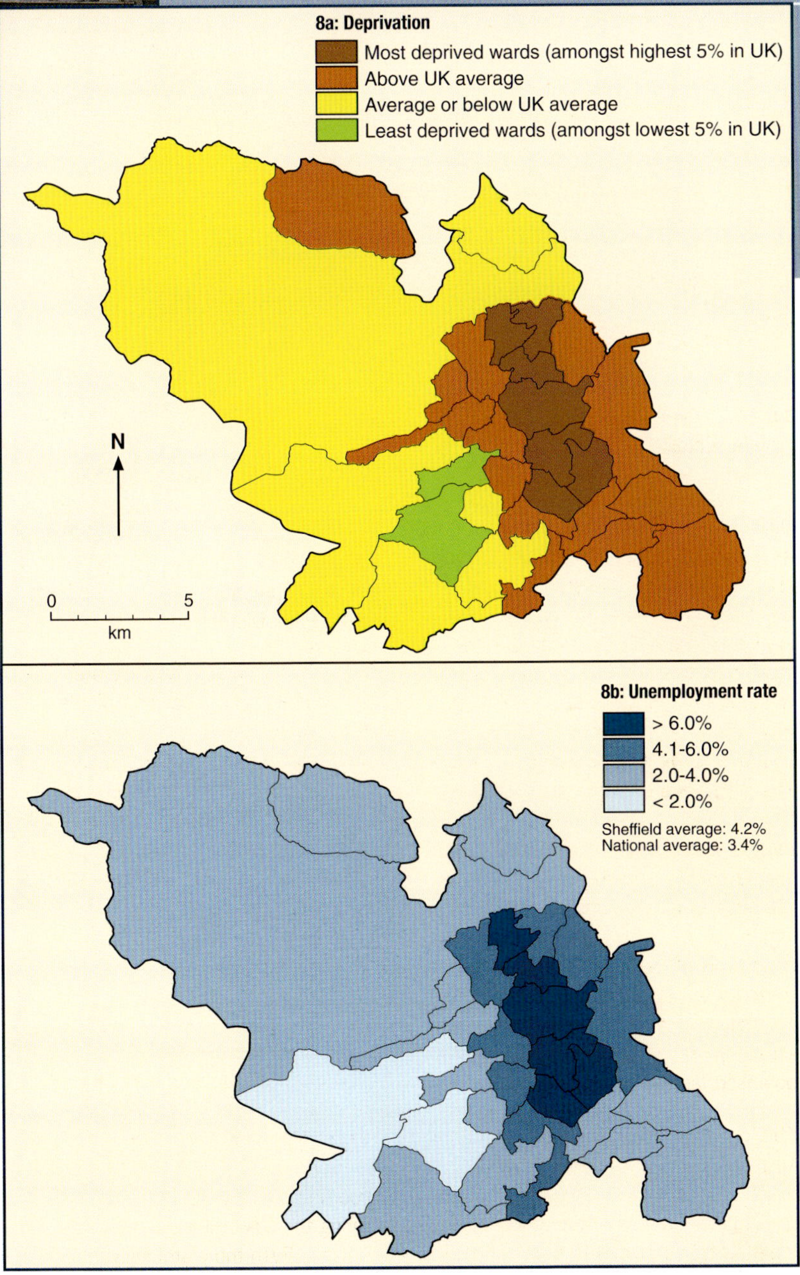

**8a: Deprivation**
- Most deprived wards (amongst highest 5% in UK)
- Above UK average
- Average or below UK average
- Least deprived wards (amongst lowest 5% in UK)

**8b: Unemployment rate**
- > 6.0%
- 4.1-6.0%
- 2.0-4.0%
- < 2.0%

Sheffield average: 4.2%
National average: 3.4%

ten years more than those in the east. Disaggregating this overall pattern highlights the very marked division within the city.

Figure 8b shows contrasts in unemployment within the city. In 2001 unemployment among those aged 16-74 ranged from over 8% in Castle and Manor to less than 2% in Ecclesall and

31

# Discovering Cities Sheffield

*Figure 8: (c) No educational qualifications figures; (d) Concentrations of council housing figures. Source: Office for National Statistics.*

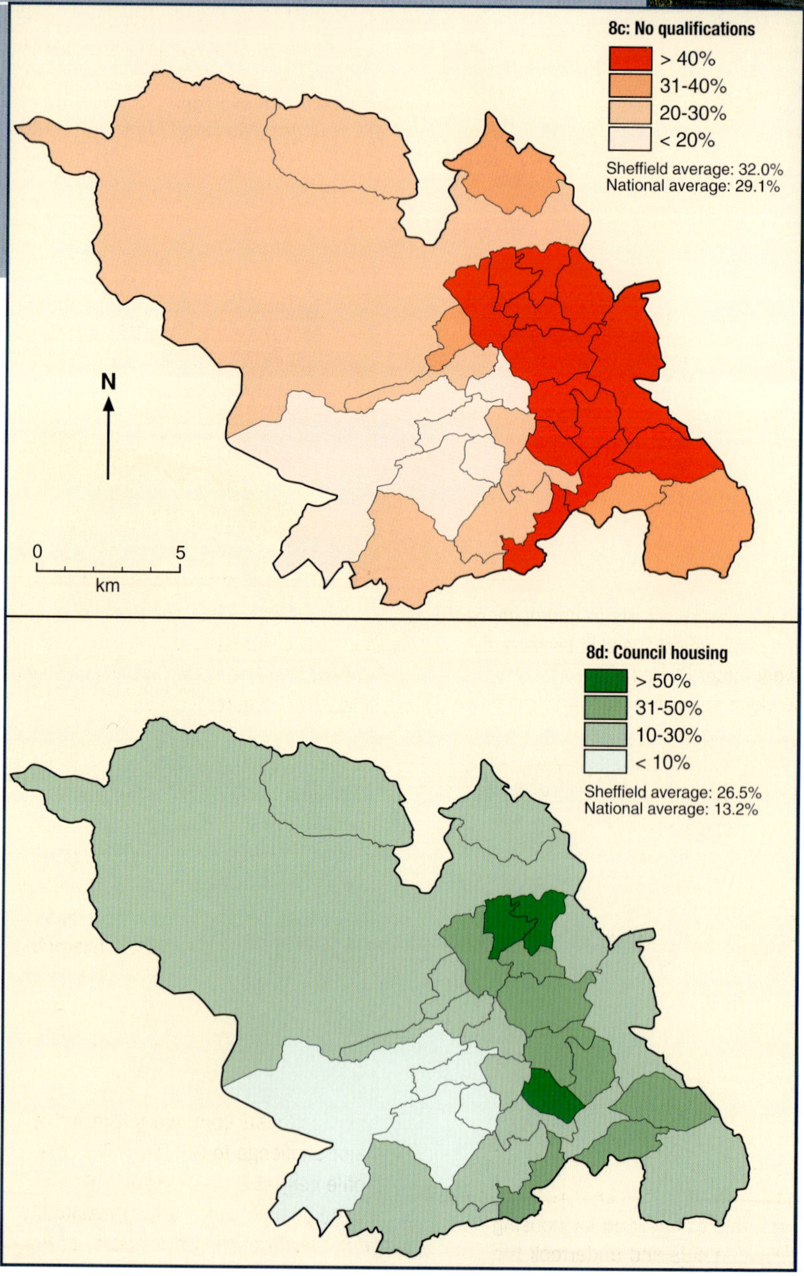

**8c: No qualifications**
- > 40%
- 31-40%
- 20-30%
- < 20%

Sheffield average: 32.0%
National average: 29.1%

**8d: Council housing**
- > 50%
- 31-50%
- 10-30%
- < 10%

Sheffield average: 26.5%
National average: 13.2%

Hallam. These figures do, of course, hide much higher rates within individual areas of the wards and among particular sections of the population. Unemployment is particularly high among older males, many of whom are also classed as long-term unemployed. The four-fold contrast in unemployment levels within a single city is a major cause for concern.

The post-industrial city

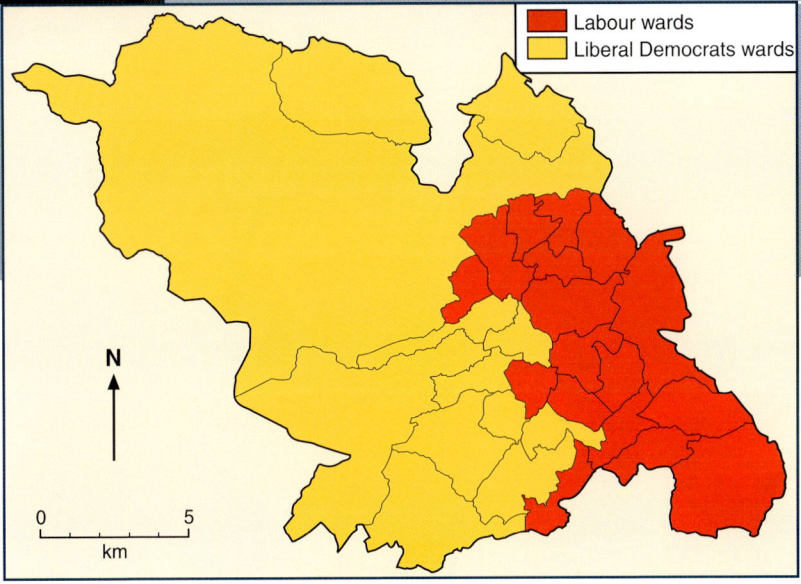

Figure 9: Outcomes of the May 2003 local elections by ward.

In part, the contrasts in unemployment may well reflect the skill levels of the work force. Overall, 32% of Sheffield's working-age population lack qualifications and the link to unemployment is made evident when Figures 8b and 8c are compared. Manor tops the list with over 50% of the working-age population lacking qualifications compared with figures of less than 16% in Ecclesall, Hallam and Nether Edge. A very low figure of 7% in Broomhill hints at the presence of large numbers of university students in this ward. Again, the most striking feature is the east-west contrast.

Although this east-west contrast is well-established, it was reinforced throughout the twentieth century by the concentration of council housing in the east (Figure 8d) where the City Council was able to buy land for housing developments and undertook the comprehensive development schemes noted earlier. An indication of the contrasts in the geographies of council housing is a figure of less than 2% in Ecclesall compared with over 60% in Southey Green.

Not surprisingly, these social and economic contrasts between the 'two Sheffields' are reflected in local political allegiances. Figure 9 shows the results of the May 2003 local elections. Labour's heartlands are to the east while the Liberal Democrats' are to the west. This makes for interesting debates, especially in spatial planning matters, where the Labour east has the final say on developments in Liberal Democrat west. One current debate, for example, is the extent to which apartment complexes can be built in the grounds of the large nineteenth-century houses in the west of the city.

These contrasts continue to present a major challenge to Sheffield. The high-profile central area developments and a strong local economy may eventually bring benefit to the poorer parts of the city. However, it is only when a prosperous economy is accompanied by a marked reduction in contrasts between east and west that Sheffield will be able to market itself as a successful European city.

Discovering Cities Sheffield

# Small area studies and trails

*The heart of the City.*

## Introduction

These three trails focus on the contemporary city and show how current patterns are tied into the past. The first two trails are concerned with the centre of Sheffield. The first focuses upon the Heart of the City project and the core of the retail area. The second is a transect across the city centre which emphasises the linear spread of the shopping area and illustrates the mixed land uses which lie just outside the commercial core. The third trail takes us through part of an area which was once the major centre of the steel industry and focuses on the new projects which occupy the sites of former steel works.

## Trail 1: Retailing and the Heart of the City

Distance: 2.75km
Walking Time (without stops): 45 minutes
Disabled access: Yes

This trail focuses on the core of the city taking in the present-day administrative, cultural and shopping centres. There is an outer area of eighteenth-century buildings (well preserved in the north, but very limited to the south) and an inner core of Victorian and modern buildings. The central part of this area is being redeveloped as the Heart of the City project, first announced in 1994 and currently being co-ordinated by Sheffield 1, an Urban Regeneration Company. It is financed both by public funds (such as the National lottery and the EU) and the private sector and is designed to give a vibrant core to the city and lead to other regeneration projects. Phase 1, consisting primarily of redevelopment of the Peace Gardens, and construction of the Winter Garden and Millennium Galleries is complete. Phase 2, which includes the construction of a hotel and office block began in November 2003.

1. The trail starts in Paradise Square (which dates mainly from 1771, and 1736 on the north side), Sheffield's only surviving eighteenth-century square and part of what is now termed the Cathedral Quarter. This is essentially an office quarter.

Small area studies and trails

*Trail 1.*

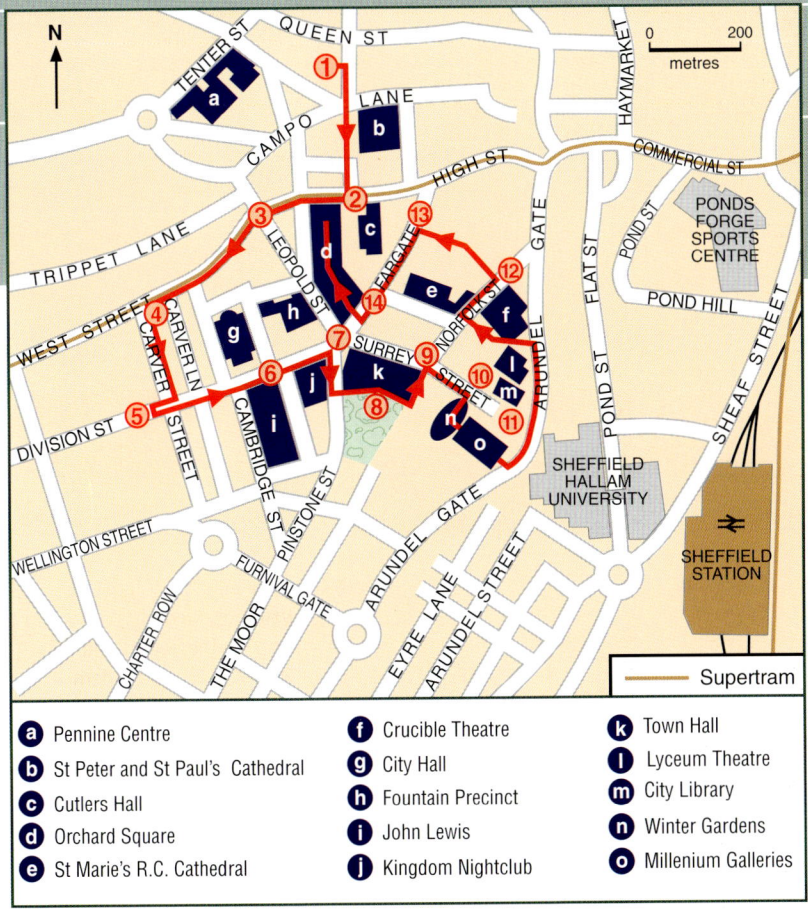

| | | | | | |
|---|---|---|---|---|---|
| **a** Pennine Centre | **f** Crucible Theatre | **k** Town Hall |
| **b** St Peter and St Paul's Cathedral | **g** City Hall | **l** Lyceum Theatre |
| **c** Cutlers Hall | **h** Fountain Precinct | **m** City Library |
| **d** Orchard Square | **i** John Lewis | **n** Winter Gardens |
| **e** St Marie's R.C. Cathedral | **j** Kingdom Nightclub | **o** Millenium Galleries |

Towering over the square to the west is the Pennine Centre, the main Sheffield office of HSBC, which was built in the 1970s. Proceed up Paradise Street to the higher land between the Don and Sheaf valleys upon which the town was founded.

2. Cross Campo Lane and then walk along St James's Row to the Cathedral forecourt, passing the Girls' Charity School on the right which is one of a number of eighteenth-century buildings still remaining. The Cathedral's most striking external feature is the west end and main entrance, which were added in the 1960s. Looking south from the main entrance of the Cathedral, immediately ahead is the Cutlers Hall, the left hand side of the building dating back to 1832. To the left of the Cutlers Hall is a Victorian bank dating from 1866 (now Royal Bank of Scotland) and to the right is the 1838 Sheffield and Hallamshire Bank (now HSBC). The Cathedral forecourt (the original graveyard was reduced in size by Victorian road widening and the recent addition of a tram stop) is framed by two distinctive brick buildings: Parade Chambers (1883) to the east and Gladstone Buildings

35

# Discovering Cities Sheffield

*Firth College.*

(1885) to the west. This area of the city was part of the commercial core of nineteenth-century Sheffield.

3. Turning right along Church Street note Cairns Chambers (1894-6) on the right, with a statue of a Lord Chancellor over the main doorway. Ahead, the junction of Leopold Street and West Street is marked by the late 1870s Firth College building. Part of the University of Sheffield was based here until it moved to its present site in 1905. The College and surrounding buildings have been used most recently as education offices and are now scheduled for a mixed-use redevelopment project. Opposite, on West Street, is Steel City House, the former telephone exchange (now offices occupied by Jobcentre Plus). Further along West Street, on the left is a former printing works (now the Reflex Bar) and on the right (next to the Co-operative Bank) Westpoint, a new city centre block of 87 apartments built on the site of a former clothing factory. These provide two examples of the ways in which parts of the inner ring of industrial premises have been transformed into residential and leisure use.

4. Turn left onto Carver Street. The Walkabout pub is a former Methodist Chapel (1804). On the left is the derelict Kendal Works, some of which dates from the 1830s. These small, domestic-scale premises are arranged around a courtyard and were formerly occupied by cutlers and associated trades. On the right is the Alpha Works (1900), which formerly produced silver plated items and is now used primarily as offices by voluntary organisations. The contrast in size between Kendal Works and Alpha Works demonstrates the changing scale of production in the lighter trades as the century progressed. Just before the junction of Carver Street and Division Street is the former National School (Dikkins) of 1812, a reminder of the high-density residential development of this area in the nineteenth century.

## Small area studies and trails

Barker's Pool.

5. Turn right onto Division Street. To the west, the vista is blocked by West One, a new complex of bars, restaurants and almost 500 apartments. It is thought to be the largest construction project in Sheffield since Meadowhall. The development was stimulated in part by the universities in that this and the 162-apartment Royal Plaza on West Street, started life as proposals for student accommodation. Walk west through the Devonshire Quarter, which is perhaps the largest and most successful area of contemporary inner-city living in Sheffield. At street level the City Council are attempting to retain a mix of half entertainment and half retail activities. Changed uses are illustrated by the former fire station of 1929 (now Bar Coast with student accommodation above). To the left is Canning Street (with some surviving back-to-back houses) and shortly beyond that, Aberdeen Court, a former small workshop complex (last used by silversmiths) turned into retail outlets.

6. Retrace your steps to Barker's Pool, noting Lloyds Number 1 bar in the former head office of the Sheffield Waterworks Company. This was built in 1867 and has been described as Sheffield's Venetian Palace! Barker's Pool takes its name from a reservoir for water storage on the edge of the eighteenth-century city. To the left is the 2700-seat City Hall (a civic project opened in 1932) and the Fountain Precinct office buildings that replaced the Grand Hotel which closed in 1971. On the right is the John Lewis department store. When the store was built in 1964, this was seen as a rather risky venture in a 'dead' area between the two shopping zones (Moor and Castle). The modern (and at the time controversial) red-framed building next to John Lewis replaced the Gaumont cinema in the late 1980s. It is currently in use as the Kingdom nightclub with retail outlets on the street level. At the end of Barker's Pool the skyline ahead is dominated by the spire of St Marie's Roman Catholic Cathedral and the Town Hall clock capped by a statue of Vulcan.

7. Turn right into Pinstone Street. The Town Hall was designed by E W Mountford and constructed mainly from 1890-1897 at the peak of the city's prosperity (the frieze around the building celebrates the city's achievements). This Town Hall

37

## Discovering Cities Sheffield

*The Winter Garden.*

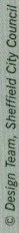
© Design Team, Sheffield City Council

replaced the previous one (see Trail 2) and marked an important southern shift in the city's activities.

8. Walk into the Peace Gardens to the right of the Town Hall. The Peace Gardens are part of the Heart of the City project. This was originally the site of St Paul's Church which was demolished in 1938 and replaced by a conventional civic park before being redeveloped. Ahead the Winter Garden can be seen. Phase 2 plans for the Heart of the City project include an office block/apartments to the right of the Winter Garden and, controversially, a new hotel which will block the view of the Winter Garden from the Peace Gardens. Millennium Square is currently (February 2004) under construction to provide a southern entrance to the Winter Garden. Cross the Peace Gardens and exit to the left along Norfolk Street.

9. Turn right into Surrey Street. The Brown Bear pub dates from 1745 and is one of a group of Georgian buildings to survive on the southern edge of the city. Ahead on the left is the Central Library and Graves Art Gallery, another 1930s civic project.

10. Enter the Winter Garden on the right. Opened in 2002, the Garden provides a striking building in the heart of the city and is claimed to be the largest temperate glasshouse in any European city. It is a development which complements the recently refurbished Botanical Gardens of 1836, situated approximately 2km south-west of the city centre. Within the Winter Garden turn left into the Millennium Galleries where it is possible to walk through and take an escalator (or lift) to the lower level. The Millennium Galleries, opened in 2001, house several permanent displays in addition to a number of visiting exhibitions each year from the Victoria and Albert and Tate collections. On leaving the Millennium Galleries, turn left along Arundel Gate. The white-tiled, unfinished end of the Central Library hints at how this road was pushed across existing street lines. To the right is the Adsetts Centre of Sheffield Hallam University and beyond that, on the eastern side of the Sheaf Valley, the Park Hill flats.

11. Turn left into Tudor Square which contains Sheffield's two theatres. The Lyceum is a venue for touring

**Small area studies and trails**

*© Millennium Galleries Sheffield*

Sheffield Theatres, Tudor Square.

*© Gerry Murray/Sheffield Theatres*

companies (ballet, opera and theatre) and has the traditional proscenium arch stage. Opened in 1893 it was rescued (partly with EU aid) from the threat of demolition in the late 1980s as part of the package of cultural developments and events linked to the World Student Games. The Crucible Theatre, with its thrust stage, was opened in 1970. It is known to many people as the location in which the World Snooker Championships are held, but is valued equally for the quality of its theatrical productions. Walk across Tudor Square noting the pedestrianised Norfolk Row ahead – another Georgian survivor on the south of the central area.

12. Turn right along Norfolk Street and enter Chapel Walk. The entrance to Chapel Walk is framed by Methodist and United Reformed chapels. This narrow street is the nearest Sheffield's city centre has to a shopping arcade (although uncovered) and is the site of some specialist boutiques. Emerging from Chapel Walk, note, beyond the tram lines to the right, the Telegraph building (completed in 1916) which fronts the printing works of the local newspapers.

13. Turn left into Fargate. Sheffield's principal shopping street is an eclectic mix of building styles and was pedestrianised in the 1970s. The larger stores tend to be on the left because the Cutlers Hall impinges to the rear of the shops on the right and constrains the amount of space for retailing purposes.

14. Turn right into Orchard Square, the only major retailing redevelopment in the city centre in the recent past. Craft shops on an upper level complement the chain stores on the lower levels, while the distinctive clock tower reminds shoppers of Sheffield's cutlery heritage every 15 minutes. Leave through the Leopold Street entrance and return to the Cathedral forecourt close to the starting point of the trail. A more direct route is available to the right of TK Maxx, but this includes a short flight of steps.

39

# Discovering Cities Sheffield

*Trail 2.*

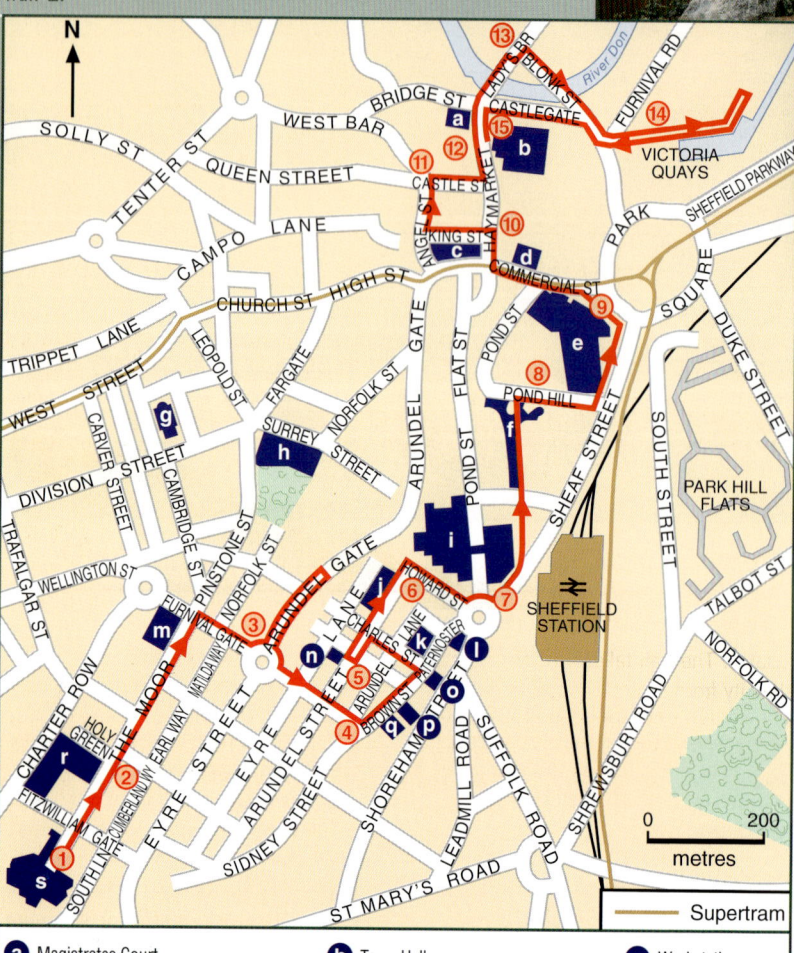

- **a** Magistrates Court
- **b** Castle Market
- **c** Primark
- **d** No.1 Restaurant
- **e** Ponds Forge International Sports Centre
- **f** Pond Street Bus Station
- **g** City Hall
- **h** Town Hall
- **i** Sheffield Hallam University
- **j** Sheffield Science & Technology Park
- **k** Former National Centre for Popular Music
- **l** Showroom Cinema
- **m** Debenhams
- **n** Butcher Wheel
- **o** Workstation
- **p** Site Gallery
- **q** Persistence Works
- **r** Atkinson's
- **s** DFES/DWP

## Trail 2: City centre transect: zones in transition

Distance: 3.4km
Walking Time (without stops): 60 minutes
Disabled access: Yes, but some cobbled surfaces in Victoria Quays

This trail is designed to do two things: to explore the mixed land uses found on the edge of the retail and commercial core of the city and to illustrate the economic policy initiatives of the City Council (for example, the Cultural Industries Quarter) and the Sheffield Development Corporation (Victoria

# Small area studies and trails

*City Centre.*

Quays). The trail takes a transect across the city from south to north, curving eastwards around the core. The one-way format of this trail, visiting both northern and southern extremities of the main shopping streets, helps to emphasise the distinctive linear form of Sheffield's central shopping district. A bus ride back to the starting point further emphasises this.

1. Start at Fitzwilliam Gate at its junction with the Moor. Known as Moorfoot, this is the southern extremity of the central shopping area. The large, red-brick office block to the south is the main central government office complex in Sheffield. It now houses offices of the Department for Work and Pensions and the Department for Education and Skills. To the north, the presence of mainly small retail units, some occupied by charity shops, indicates the edge of the shopping area. The Moor was once a main traffic artery, but planning initiatives changed this to a pedestrianised shopping street with market stalls along the centre. Architecturally there is a 1950s and 1960s uniformity here as many buildings were constructed to replace severely bomb-damaged ones.

2. Walk up the Moor to Holy Green. Atkinson's, on the left, was destroyed with a direct hit by a bomb in the Second World War. For the whole length to Furnival Gate not a single pre-war building survives. Some chain stores have withdrawn from this part of the shopping area, particularly since the opening of Meadowhall (see page 23). Sainsbury's Central occupies the former Marks and Spencer site. The status of the shops increases along the Moor until at the northern end (Moorhead) the Debenhams store is reached. At Debenhams turn right along Furnival Gate and then left along Arundel Gate.

# Discovering Cities Sheffield

*Workstation, Paternoster Row.*

3. Furnival Gate and Arundel Gate were designed as part of a 1960s civic circle ring road. This was never completed, as public opinion here, as elsewhere, began to question the role of the vehicle in the city centre. The road has now been downgraded so that it forms less of a pedestrian barrier. The wide grass section in the middle of Arundel Gate marks a former road alignment which tunnelled under the adjacent roundabout. Cross to the other side of Arundel Gate and note the marked transition between the new Stoddart Building of Sheffield Hallam University (on the left) and the surviving industrial land uses to the right.

4. Continue down to Brown Street and the Sheaf Valley. For most of its route through the centre of Sheffield the Sheaf is in a culvert, part of which runs under the railway station. The Cultural Industries Quarter (focused upon Brown Street and Paternoster Row) has been encouraged by the City Council from the late 1980s. On the right hand side are the Persistence Works (a purpose-built art and craft studio complex), the Site Gallery and the Workstation. The Workstation, opened in 1993, provides over 21,000sqm of work space for 50 media companies. The row of 'cultural buildings', converted from a 1936 Art Deco car dealership, culminates in the Showroom independent cinema. On Shoreham Street are the Council-run Red Tape recording studios and BBC Radio Sheffield. It seems reasonable to assume that these developments have contributed to the fact that 7% of Sheffield's working population are employed in creative industries compared with a national average of 4%. These figures would also include those employed in the writing of software for computer games for which Sheffield has an international reputation. On the left, with four stainless steel drums (planned to become Sheffield Hallam University's Students' Union building) is the former National Centre of Popular Music (see page 21).

5. Turn left along Charles Street and left again at the junction with Arundel Street. Butcher Wheel (72 Arundel Street) once made edge tools. It is a large and atmospheric group of buildings arranged around a courtyard and typical of the larger industrial buildings which once occupied this part of the town.

**Small area studies and trails**

*The Old Queen's Head*

Returning to Charles Street and walking to the north, note the Cooper Building which is the city centre site of Sheffield Technology Parks (STP), a City Council initiative to encourage the start-up of new companies. The building originally housed a manufacturer of mother-of-pearl handles for cutlery but now comprises office units.

6. Proceed down Howard Street. On the right is Sheffield Hallam University Science Park, which houses a selection of research units together with the offices of the firm that operates a combined heat and power system in the city. To the left are the main buildings of Sheffield Hallam University. The 11-storey Owen Building (built in the late 1950s) was originally the College of Technology which formed a key part of this university.

7. Turn left along Sheaf Street. The railway station frontage dates from 1905. The main road is a barrier between the station and the rest of the city. Current plans envisage a new square here and a downgraded Sheaf Street. It is hoped the square will solve a long-standing problem of providing a welcoming and pedestrian-friendly route to the city centre. In the 1960s it was hoped to divert Sheaf Street traffic to the east of the station but cost considerations ruled this out.

8. Take the signed route to the Transport Interchange and then turn right into Pond Hill. The Old Queen's Head, on the right, is a late fifteenth century, timber-framed building. It is the only medieval building other than the Cathedral to remain in central Sheffield. On the left of Pond Hill is Aspect Court which is one of the Sheffield sites occupied by the Home Office. Just beyond is the (re-located) gateway of the Ponds Forge steelworks which closed in 1968.

9. Walk round the Ponds Forge International Sports Centre. The sports centre has an Olympic-standard 50m pool and diving pool, with seating for over 3000, a sports hall and leisure facilities. Continue up Commercial Street. On the left the former Barclays Bank is being converted into 56 apartments and on the right the former Gas Offices (1874), built in the classical style of a grand Italian villa, are now No. 1, a Chinese Restaurant.

10. Turn right into Haymarket, the entrance to the Castlegate area. Castlegate (the northern extremity of the central shopping streets) is an area in transition and for which it is proving difficult to find a role. Several department stores have left

## Discovering Cities Sheffield

*Castle Street brickwork.*

© Diane Wright

the area, including Woolworths and BhS. This is also a key site as it is the gateway to Sheffield from the Parkway link from the M1. Several redevelopment projects have failed to materialise and at least one major building has offered an 'exciting refurbishment opportunity' for a number of years. Turn left into King Street. On the left the Primark store is on the site of the Victorian Fitzalan Market Hall and adjacent to the site of the medieval market cross.

11. Turn right into Angel Street. This is the most successful of the regeneration projects within the Castlegate area, and is the site of a department store (the Co-op in Castle House), an Argos superstore and a new Travel Inn, one of Sheffield's many new hotels.

12. Turn right into Castle Street, where an end-wall mosaic of a steel worker reminds us of Sheffield's heritage. Castle Market (on the site of Sheffield Castle at the end of Castle Street) survives as an example of early 1960s design, but some of the older parts of the site date back to the 1930s. It is a mixture of open market hall and covered shops. Its future is uncertain because of the cost of bringing it up to modern standards. Turn left into Waingate and walk downhill towards the River Don. Immediately on the left hand side of Waingate is the old Town Hall (currently empty) which until recently was used as the Crown Court. The Court has now moved to a new building on West Bar. Further to the left along Bridge Street are the Magistrates Court and the South Yorkshire Police headquarters. Traffic conditions are very difficult here and it is best to cross Lady's Bridge on the right hand side.

13. Looking north from Lady's Bridge, on the left are the former Exchange Brewery, now converted to offices, beyond that a vacant site scheduled for office development, and in the distance the new Riverside Exchange apartments. On the right are the new City Wharf apartments. Both apartment developments are capitalising on contemporary demand for waterfront locations. Along the Wicker are the Wicker Arches (1849), which once carried a Sheffield to Manchester railway. The Arches mark the beginning of

## Small area studies and trails

*Victoria Quays.*

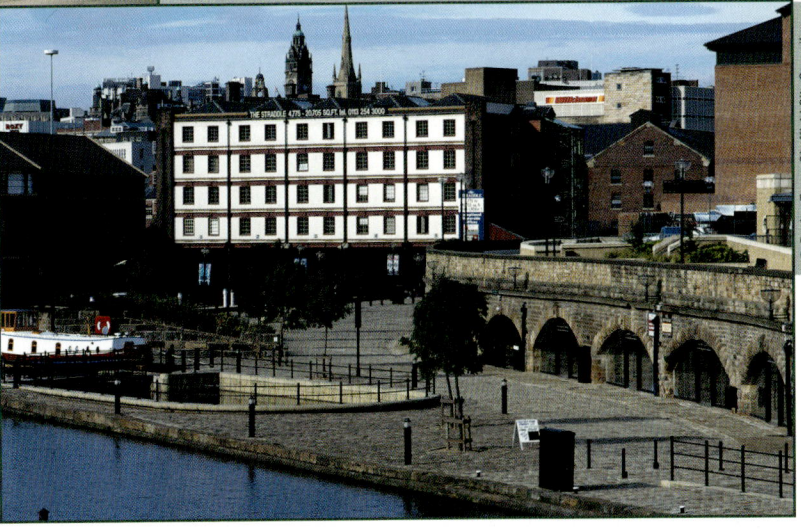

the Lower Don industrial area (see Trail 3). The area between Lady's Bridge and the Wicker Arches is likely to change dramatically in a few years' time on the completion of the northern section of the inner ring road, which will bisect the area. It will also allow the development of a more pedestrian-friendly environment in this location.
Walk along Blonk Street, noting the beginning of the Five Weirs Walk along the River Don (see Trail 3). Just beyond this point the River Sheaf (in a culvert) joins the Don. The Bristol Hotel (on the left) is converted from a former office block and, at the top of a long drive, the Holiday Inn is a former railway hotel dating from 1861.

14. Cross Furnival Road. Victoria Quays, which is accessed by a low arch, is the result of a major regeneration project in which SDC provided a lead but its isolation from the rest of the city remains a problem. Completion of the inner ring road will allow easier movement into and out of the area. The canal basin is surrounded by yet another new hotel (Hilton) and office blocks (one occupied by a major legal firm), and both the terminal warehouse (opened in 1819 at the same time as the canal) and the Straddle warehouse (1895) have been renovated for either office or residential use. At the northern end of the canal basin is the 1823 Sheaf House. This originated as the offices of Sheffield's first self-contained factory making its own steel, cutlery and edge tools. The office block is currently used as a call centre, employing 300 staff.

15. Retrace your steps, leave the canal basin by the point of entry and proceed along Castlegate. Castlegate was the site of the original livestock slaughtering yards from which waste entered the River Don. Turn left into Waingate and catch a 97 or 97A bus which will return you to the junction of Fitzwilliam Gate and Moorfoot. Do not pick up the bus on Castlegate as this will take you out of town!

**Discovering Cities Sheffield**

*Don Valley.*

## Trail 3: The Lower Don Valley

Distance: 4.75km
Walking Time (without stops): 70 minutes
Disabled access: Yes, but wheelchair users may need a radar key for the cycle gates on the Five Weirs Walk

A walk through the Lower Don Valley illustrates the ways in which traditional metal-working sites have been converted into areas of entertainment, sports and modern business parks. It also includes examples of the older industries and an area which was once one of the most important suburban shopping centres in Sheffield. Visitors wishing to go to Meadowhall may catch a tram direct to the shopping centre from the start/end point of the trail. Most of the central sections of this trail are within the area of the former SDC.

1. The trail begins at the Attercliffe tram stop adjacent to the out-of-centre site of Sheffield Science and Technology Parks, the partner of the site visited in Trail 2. In contrast to the city centre site, this site offers facilities for technology companies in modern, purpose-built, commercial premises. The signs at the entrance to each unit give an up-to-date picture of current activities.

2. Walk along Shortridge Street to Attercliffe Road. Attercliffe was once a major suburban shopping centre for the densely-packed terraced housing serving the steel works. The urban fabric shows signs of the area's past. The large white building at the junction of Shortridge Street and Attercliffe Road is the former Banner's department store. Although most residential properties have now been demolished, a number of shops are still linked to the Asian communities which moved into Attercliffe in the post-war period to work in the steel industry. Turn right, cross the road and walk north-east, observing the mixed land uses and noting former bank buildings indicative of this area's former importance.

3. Before turning left into Attercliffe

# Small area studies and trails

*Trail 3.*

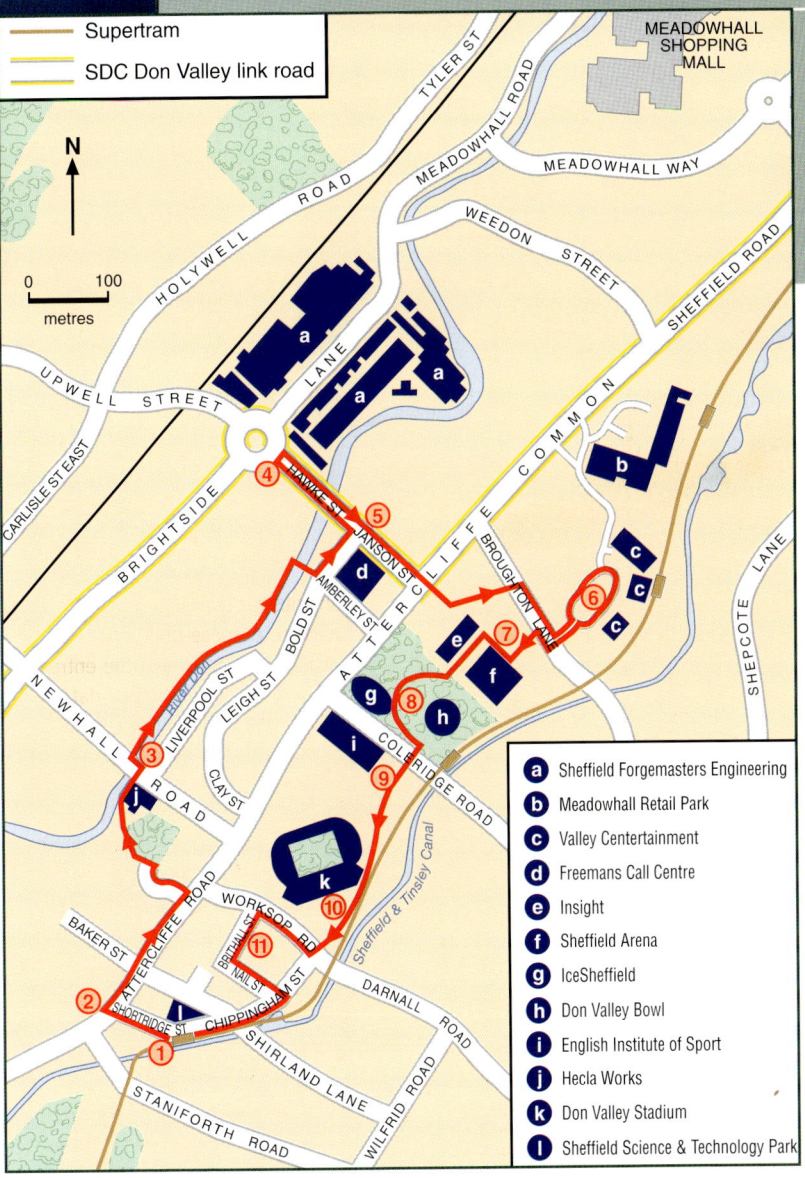

© Sheffield International Venues Ltd

**Legend:**
- Supertram
- SDC Don Valley link road

**Locations:**
- **a** Sheffield Forgemasters Engineering
- **b** Meadowhall Retail Park
- **c** Valley Centertainment
- **d** Freemans Call Centre
- **e** Insight
- **f** Sheffield Arena
- **g** IceSheffield
- **h** Don Valley Bowl
- **i** English Institute of Sport
- **j** Hecla Works
- **k** Don Valley Stadium
- **l** Sheffield Science & Technology Park

cemetery (the site of Attercliffe Church destroyed in the Second World War) note the early twentieth century Boots branch on the corner of Worksop Road, now a restaurant. Keeping to the left side of the graveyard the path leads to the river. Five Weirs Walk along the River Don has been developed over the last decade to provide a walk from the city centre (Trail 1) to Meadowhall. On the right, as the path is followed downstream, note the surviving sections of the Hecla Works, within which manganese steel was developed (see page 11). Cross the

47

# Discovering Cities Sheffield

*Modern Steelworks.*

river by the Newhall Road bridge and then continue along the north side of the river. This next section of the Five Weirs Walk was built as part of an SDC land reclamation scheme. It passes Riverside Court and a number of new industrial and commercial units which are typical of those which fill the industrial sections of the redeveloped Lower Don Valley.

4. Cross the river on the new footbridge, then turn left into Bold Street and left again into Hawke Street to the junction with Brightside Lane. Brightside Lane bisects one of Sheffield's surviving large metal plants, the River Don Works of Sheffield Forgemasters Engineering. In the late 1970s this site employed almost 2500 people. Today, owned by a foreign multinational, it produces large (up to 290,000kg) heat-treated and machined forgings and castings and its facilities include one of the world's largest forging presses. The company from which this operation is descended once owned over 4000 homes (all now cleared) in the Lower Don Valley. Brightside Lane (looking north) is the best surviving example of the 'steel canyons' which once lined the Lower Don Valley. To the left, a short way along, are the granite-faced former head offices of the River Don Works (currently awaiting new use).

5. Retrace your steps along Janson Street, which forms part of the SDC-financed Don Valley link road. A large Naval Ordnance Depot for assessing the quality of the metals used in the production of guns and armour plate was sited on the area to the right of Janson Street. The site is now occupied by the call centre of the catalogue company Freemans. Office developments like this were encouraged by SDC much to the dismay of the City Council which saw the demand for office space in the city centre fall. A budget hotel faces Arena Square. On the other side of the square is a former school but, as a result of the policy of clearing housing from the Lower Don, not a house in sight.

6. A short-cut across the Arena car park leads to Centertainment, another SDC-led development which has replaced a railway goods yard. The Noose and Gibbet at the entrance to the development was once The Railway Tavern. This out-of-centre entertainment complex with restaurants, cinemas and bowling alley is aimed at car owners but is also supported by its own tram stop. The development here

## Small area studies and trails

*Don Valley Stadium.*

may have contributed to the decline in the number of cinemas in the city centre and, like the office developments, it was not welcomed by the City Council. Architecturally it seems little more than a collection of sheds in a large car park but this belies the atmosphere inside the buildings, whether Old Orleans Diner or Hollywood Bowl. To the north of this site is the Meadowhall Retail Park (a facility distinct from the Meadowhall shopping centre), the development of which also involved a clash with the City Council.

7. Retrace your steps and cross Broughton Lane to the Hallam FM Arena. The Arena was built in 1991 for indoor events at the World Student Games and is now a multi-purpose venue. This is in the part of the Lower Don Valley developed by the City Council, not the SDC, using mainly public funds initially, Council funds and EU monies and, more recently, National Lottery funding). The World Student Games kick-started Sheffield's interest in developing a niche as a city of sport, and the facilities built for the Games (most of which are built on the site of the Brown Bayley steel works) strengthened Sheffield's claim to be a centre for sporting excellence in the UK. They were a factor in attracting to Sheffield a new tranche of facilities in 2003. To the right of the Arena is Insight, a call centre for on-line sales of computer equipment, which occupies a building formerly used as a nightclub. It is an interesting example of both the versatility of these 'sheds' and the fact that not all out-of-centre ventures succeed – indeed, the club's licence was transferred to the city centre Kingdom nightclub (see Trail 1). Walking between the Arena and Insight follow the path round with the Don Valley Bowl on the left and iceSheffield on the right.

8. The Don Valley Bowl is used for open air events such as pop concerts and firework displays. iceSheffield (opened in 2003, costing almost £16 million and funded mainly by the National Lottery) has two Olympic-size ice pads. The performance pad has seating for 1500. Follow the path round but remain inside the metal fencing to give direct access to the pedestrian/cycle bridge over Coleridge Road.

9. The £24 million regional (Yorkshire) centre of the Lottery-funded English Institute of Sport (opened in 2003) can be seen from the footbridge, to

# Discovering Cities Sheffield

*Sporting events in Sheffield.*

the left of Coleridge Road. Located in Sheffield because of its earlier commitment to sport in the World Student Games, this is one of nine planned Regional Sports Centres, each with their own specialisms. As Sheffield's main specialism is athletics, the centre contains both 200m circuit and 130m sprint tracks, jumping and throwing areas, supported by coaching facilities and departments for sports science and sports medicine. Athletics facilities are complemented by those for boxing, judo, netball, table tennis and badminton. A lack of on-site residences makes it difficult for those beyond a comfortable commuting distance to use the facilities. Continue along the path towards Don Valley Stadium. On the right is a sundial memorial to Harry Brearley, the inventor of stainless steel.

10. The Don Valley Stadium, with running tracks and field sports facilities, provides covered seating for 10,000 spectators and open terraces for a further 30,000 spectators. It is the home of Sheffield Eagles Rugby League Club and host to international and national athletics meetings. Gate N provides a reasonable view of the interior of the stadium. At this point it is worth reflecting on your own responses to these twenty-first century urban forms. Except during times when major events are taking place at one of the facilities, this, like the Five Weirs Walk, is an under-peopled landscape. Turn right on Worksop Road (noting to the left, beyond the tram bridge, the aqueduct of the Sheffield canal) and walk up Britnall Street.

11. Britnall Street is one of the first examples of the return of housing to Lower Don Valley. With industry no longer dominant the logic for the removal of residential properties is no longer justified. Significantly, a steam hammer has been placed as a centre-piece of the development. The new housing will be largely on areas formerly used for housing since much of the rest of the land is still classed as polluted after nearly 200 years of industrial use. Britnall Street leads back to the Science and Technology Park and the start of the trail.

# Bibliography and further information

Barraclough, K.C. (1976) *Sheffield Steel*. Ashbourne: Moorland Publishing.

Bayliss, D. (ed) (1995) *A Guide to the Industrial History of South Yorkshire*. Sheffield: Association of Industrial Archaeology.

Beedham, A. (2003) *Peeks at the Past in Sheffield and the Surrounding Area*. Sheffield: Pickard Publishing.

Binfield, C., Childs, R., Harper, R., Hey, D., Martin, D. and Tweedale, G. (eds) (1993) *The History of the City of Sheffield 1843-1993* (3 volumes). Sheffield: Sheffield Academic Press.

Binfield, C. and Hey, D. (1997) *Mesters to Masters: A history of the Company of Cutlers in Hallamshire*. Oxford: Oxford University Press.

Fine, D. (2003) *Sheffield: History and Guide*. Stroud: Tempus Publishing.

Griffiths, P. (1999) *The Five Weirs Walk. Sheffield East End history trail 3*. Sheffield: The Hallamshire Press.

Harman, R. and Ogden, S. (1997) *The Attercliffe Village Trail: Sheffield East End history trail 2*. Sheffield: The Hallamshire Press.

Hey, D. (1979) *The Making of South Yorkshire*. Ashbourne: Moorland Publishing.

Hey, D. (1998) *A History of Sheffield*. Lancaster: Carnegie Publishing.

Hey, D., Olive, M. and Liddament, D. (1997) *The Forging of the Valley*. Sheffield: Sheffield Academic Press.

Jones, M. (2000) *The Making of the South Yorkshire Landscape*. Barnsley: Wharncliffe Books.

Josvig, H. (1968) *Sheffield-Rotherham*. Freiburg: Geographischen Institute der Albert-Ludwigs Universitat.

Linton, D.L. (ed) (1956) *Sheffield and its Region*. Sheffield: British Association.

Ogden, S. (1997) *The Sheffield and Tinsley Canal. Sheffield East End history trail 1*. Sheffield: The Hallamshire Press.

Pevsner, N. (1967) *The Buildings of England: Yorkshire West Riding*. Harmondsworth: Penguin.

Reid, G. (2001) *Sheffield and its Electoral Wards: A review of the Index of Multiple Deprivation, 2000*. Sheffield: Sheffield Health Authority (available at www.sheffield.nhs.uk/reports).

Sheffield City Council (2003) *Sheffield City Strategy 2002-5*. Sheffield: Sheffield City Council

SheffieldFirst (2003) *Creative Sheffield: Prospectus for a distinctive European city in a prosperous region*. Sheffield: SheffieldFirst.

Tweedale, G. (1986) *Giants of Sheffield Steel*. Sheffield: Sheffield City Libraries.

Tweedale, G. (1995) *Steel City: Entrepreneurship, strategy and technology in Sheffield 1743-1993*. Oxford: Clarendon Press.

Wagstaff, N. (2002) *Sheffield: Official city guide*. Sheffield: Sheffield City Council.

Watts, H.D., Smithson, P.A. and White, P.E. (1989) *Sheffield Today: An introduction and guide*. Sheffield: Department of Geography, University of Sheffield.

West, B.A. (1998) *Listed Buildings in Sheffield*. Sheffield: Hallamshire Press.

Wray, N., Hawkins, B. and Giles, C. (2001) *One Great Workshop: The buildings of the Sheffield metal trades*. London: English Heritage.

**Further Information**
Sheffield Tourism Services
(Postal or telephone enquiries only)
Blades Enterprise Centre, John Street
Tel: 0114 221 1900

**Maps**
Landranger 110 Sheffield and Huddersfield (1: 50,000)
Landranger 111 Sheffield and Doncaster (1: 50,000)
A-Z Map Company Ltd *A-Z Sheffield* (1: 18, 103)

**Local Studies Library**
Sheffield Central Library, Surrey Street
Tel: 0114 273 4753

**Museums**
Shepherd Wheel
Whiteley Woods
Tel: 0114 236 7731

Abbeydale Industrial Hamlet
Abbeydale Road South
Tel: 0114 236 7731

Kelham Island Museum
Kelham Island
Tel: 0114 272 2106

Magna Science Adventure Centre
Sheffield Road
Rotherham
Tel: 01709 720000

# Photo credits

**Websites**

Cultural Industries Quarter
www.ciq.org.uk

English Institute of Sport
www.eis2win.co.uk

Made in Sheffield Dot Com
www.made-in-sheffield.com

Sheffield Botanical Gardens
www.sbg.org.uk

Sheffield City Council
www.sheffield.gov.uk

SheffieldFirst Partnership
www.sheffieldfirst.com

Sheffield Galleries and Museums Trust
www.sheffieldgalleries.org.uk

Sheffield International Venues
www.sivltd.co.uk

Sheffield Industrial Museums Trust
www.simt.co.uk

Sheffield Science and Technology Parks
www.sci-tech.org.uk

Sheffield Star
www.sheffieldtoday.net

Sheffield Tourism Services
www.sheffieldcity.co.uk

South Yorkshire Objective 1 Directorate
www.goyh.gov.uk/objective1

Yorkshire Forward
www.yorkshire-forward.com

The GA would like to thank the following for their help with photographs for this book:

- Anna Gunby
- A.P.S. (UK)
- Design Team, Sheffield City Council
- Diane Wright
- Feilden Clegg Bradley Architects
- Hedgerow Publishing Ltd
- Meadowhall Management
- Millennium Galleries
- Paul White Photography/Carey Jones Architects
- Sheffield Industrial Museums Trust
- Sheffield International Venues Ltd
- Sheffield Libraries Archive and Information; Local Studies
- Sheffield Theatres
- Stagecoach Supertram
- Showroom & Workstation
- University of Sheffield